ONE MOMENT TO MIDNIGHT

We ought to obey God rather than men

Nov. 5/04

To Annelore
with love,
Erika

Erika Kubassek

ONE MOMENT TO MIDNIGHT

We ought to obey God rather than men

Erika Kubassek

PUBLISHED BY:
BRENTWOOD CHRISTIAN PRESS
4000 BEALLWOOD AVENUE
COLUMBUS, GEORGIA 31904

Dedication

Jesus, the Same
Yesterday, today, and forever
He still saves, heals and
Sends today

In Memory
Of my beloved parents
Irmgard and Ernst Kretschman

Many thanks to my dear friend
Laureen Eby
For all her help and friendship

Contents

CHAPTER ONE

The Millenium

In May of the Millenium year 2000, the Lord commanded me to take a letter with a message to the Members of the American Congress in Washington, D.C.

Accompanied by a Christian lady friend, I drove down to Washington. The bright and sunny day did not match the gloomy message we carried. As a columnist for a Christian paper based in Toronto, I was in possession of a press badge. Using this pass, I entered the office block across the street from the Capitol building. There I delivered copies of the letter to the senators' offices.

The letter was addressed to the Members of the American Congress, as follows:

May 16, 2000.

To all Members of the
American Congress,
Capitol Hill,
Washington, D.C.
U.S.A.

Gentlemen/Ladies:
Re: Vermont Decision allowing Gay Marriage

Recently, the Vermont House of Representatives passed a bill granting the full benefits of marriage to same-sex couples.

This bill would allow same sex civil unions. In other words, Vermont would allow homosexual marriages by July 1, 2000.

This decision, to recognize same-sex couples allowing them to marry was a fatal error. The moral laws given to our forefathers, based on the Holy Bible, still apply today.

God did not spare Sodom and Gomorrah, and He will not spare America, or any other country, that breaks His moral laws. Such countries are doomed.

Holy Scripture reveals that the LORD abhors the homosexual lifestyle – and indeed all immorality. It doesn't matter what people think or want – it matters only what the LORD GOD thinks.

The consequences of disobedience to God's laws are severe.

The disaster of Los Alamos is only a small foretaste of the judgment to come.

Erika Kubassek
Prophetess of the LORD

Later, after attending a press conference on the lawn in front of the Capitol buildings, I got the opportunity to meet up with Democrat Senator Tom Daschle. Introducing myself to him as we shook hands, I told him I was concerned that the US state of Vermont, now performs gay marriages. "You know," I said, "In history, the LORD always sent judgment to nations that broke His moral laws. There may be nuclear bombs used." As I was walking away from him, he just stared at me.

My friend and I then left Washington – our mission accomplished.

When the USA was attacked by Muslim terrorists on September 11, 2001, the first part of my prophecy came to pass. New York also happens to be the city where the blasphemous play, "The Last Temptation of Christ" was performed off broadway, it was the city that bore the brunt of the terror attacks, which brought down the twin Trade Towers in Manhattan. God's Word says: "They sow to the wind and reap the whirlwind." (Hosea 8:7)

The Calling and the Mission

"Open your mouth wide and I will fill it," was the prophecy given to me at my baptism through Brother Eric, who was serving as a prophet in my church on January 2, 1977. And now, the Lord said to me, "Go and I will send you to the political leaders and press, and will give you what you must say to them."

"The measure is almost full. There is only a short grace period left before I will judge the earth," said the Lord.

Isaiah, the prophet, spoke these words and they ring true today. "And judgment is turned away backward, and justice stands afar off. For truth is fallen in the street and equity cannot enter. Yea, truth falls and he that departs from evil makes himself a prey. And the Lord saw it, and it displeased him that there was no judgment." Isaiah 59: 14,15

Two years after I was baptized on one night in November 1979, I was experiencing breathing problems and desperately prayed to the Lord for help; when I heard a voice say to me, "I am Jesus, know this, I am reaching out to you." Suddenly a strong electric power started at the top of my head and went right through my body to my legs. When it stopped, I began to pray with such power and volume, as if my voice was amplified with the use of a microphone. My husband, Phil, came running into my bedroom and studied me for a few moments, said, "You have received the Holy Spirit." He had experienced this before, but I certainly did not know what was happening to me. The Bible, of course, tells us that, "We will receive power from on high when the Holy Spirit will come upon us and be witnesses for God." (Acts 1:8.) Under the impression that God did not reveal Himself to people in these ways anymore, I was totally stunned. Now I could feel the power of God in my spirit. Daily the Lord communicated with me. The gifts of tongues, revelations, (seeing in the Spirit) the word of knowledge, interpretation and prophecy, as well as a singing voice, and singing in the Spirit, were special gifts I received. God's Spirit began to teach me in wondrous ways, and the Bible became easier to understand.

At one point the Lord said, "I will make you to see through the walls of this house." I literally expected to see through them as if looking through glass. It was only later that I understood what the Lord meant. He would give me a vision for our city, our country, and indeed, the world. After this visitation from the Lord, both my husband and I were called into ministry. We were to bring prophetic messages to politicians and the press regarding the moral decay of our time.

Put on sackcloth, O priests and mourn;
Wail, you who minister before the altar
What a dreadful day!
For the day of the Lord is near;
It will come like a destruction from
The Almighty

Joel: 13,15

Israel 1980

In the fall of 1980, God opened the way for me to go to Israel for a Bible course. The church we belonged to, was operating a Christian kibbutz with fruit orchards, vineyards, grain fields, and produce gardens. One wonderful month went by quickly at Zikhron Yaaqov, near Haifa, on the Mediterranean coast. I could not get enough of the fragrant air, the warm climate, the multitude of plants, flowers, birds, and the Mediterranean Sea, which shimmered like blue sapphire jewels.

The two elderly sisters who ran this kibbutz, were endowed with spiritual gifts and allowed me to exercise mine in the congregation. Finding out how blessed the Christian life can be worshipping, singing, working and eating together, was a new surprise to me. I had not experienced such a wonderful atmosphere of peace, unity and cooperation anywhere before. The presence of the Lord was palpable. I learned how exhilarating it was to know that the Bible was truly the Word of God, and that we have a future with Him. After visiting Jerusalem by bus, and seeing some of the sights, I returned home to Canada filled with joy, expectation, and triumphantly glad that I had found my way with the Lord.

My Roots

My husband Phil and I met in 1976, at the Christian Community Church of the Brethren, near Washington, Ontario. This large farm was founded by Phil's father in the forties. His dad was the Minister as well, and held Church services until his death in 1961. Phil's mother, the matriarch of the Community Farm, bore fifteen children; Phil was the fourth son with eight sisters and six brothers. Today, several of his siblings still remain on the farm. The rest are dispersed in the USA and Canada. Three of them have now passed on.

I, in turn, come from a small family. In 1957 when I was in my teens, we moved from post-war Germany to Canada. My mother, father, older sister, and I, including my maternal grandmother, were an extremely close-knit family. After attending community college for business training and learning English, I went to work at an office in Hamilton.

Some years later, now in my early thirties, my father who was Baptist, took me to the Community Farm Church services. He told me the Lord reveals Himself through spiritual gifts in the church. Some time later, I met Phil.

Since I was unable to handle heavy work, I could not become part of this farm community, so Phil decided to leave. Shortly, thereafter, we were married at the Central Baptist Church in Kitchener. We resided in that city for the next fourteen years. Because Phil grew up on his family's farm, he was trained only in farming, and at that time, was operating a factory, one of the farm's businesses, which manufactured egg noodles. While in Kitchener, he had to take a simple job in the city. However, we had great faith in the LORD to take care of us. And, He did.

And, now back from Israel, Aunt Ruth, my father's sister, wife of a Baptist pastor of a large congregation in Berlin, telephoned me from Germany. She said, "I have a message for you from the Lord: Look up Judges 5:7 in the Bible." Translated from the German Luther Bible, the passage read: "The leadership failed in Israel, until I Deborah arose, until I arose, a mother in Israel." My aunt reiterated that she was sure that this message was for me. Thanking her for phoning me, I was filled with joyful surprise. Here, was the confirmation for my prophetic calling from the LORD. Later I received a letter from my aunt confirming her phone call from Europe. How marvelous are God's ways with His children!

The following year, in 1981, I returned to Zikhron Yaaqov, Israel, for another Bible course. This time the Lord spoke through scripture, *"You are my witnesses, that I am God."* This is the theme I felt God was speaking about in Isaiah Chapter 43. Indescribable bliss, unspeakable wonder, and blessing, flowed through my entire being as this was revealed to me.

The Work Begins

Upon my return from Israel, the Lord commanded me to "Go help the women in the YWCA." A short time later, I started a counseling ministry, where some women came with emotional and financial needs. After meeting with some of them, I realized the necessity for Christian ministry in the YWCA of downtown Kitchener. Some of these women had been treated very roughly indeed. Some had experienced nervous breakdowns due to marriage failures, and lost their children and families. They were in emotional turmoil, and were financially poor.

One day I received a telephone call from a man named Roman who was from Cuba, but was now living in Kitchener. He had experienced a dramatic conversion from Communism to Christianity. "Would you consider doing counseling for us?" he asked. That was the beginning of my work with the 700 Club's Operation Blessing, Kitchener. Subsequently, Operation Blessing opened a large store where household items and clothing were given to the poor in our community.

One of the big problems facing single women at that time was a lack of affordable housing. Again and again, I met women who complained that they had no place to live. Of course, without an address, they could not get social assistance, and without money, they could not get a place to live. It was an impossible situation. If they were on the street, unless someone helped them, they were down and out. At that time, I thought, if I hear of another woman who has to live on the street, I will go out and rent a house for women to live in. Sure enough, that day came very quickly.

Compassion overwhelmed me when I met a teenage girl at Operation Blessing, who said she had no where to sleep that night. I made up my mind right then to go house hunting. Together with Sandra, one of the young women I knew from the YWCA, we went looking for a house. We found a big old home on Joseph Street in Kitchener, over looking Victoria Park. "Let's take it," Sandra said. That settled it. My husband, Phil, was surprisingly easy to convince, but neither one of us realized what a big undertaking it would prove to be.

House of Zion

Moving day came and went. In a short time the new house was filled with residents. One resident was an English woman in her early thirties, who, because of her husband's infidelity and cruelty, suffered a nervous breakdown. Due to her illness, the two children had been taken away from her, by the Family and Childrens Services. Another woman came from a dysfunctional family where alcoholism and sexual abuse were present. An eighteen year old black, single, mother came with her two year old child. Another lady in her late sixties also came to live with us, who would cook large pots of delicious stew for residents and visitors. Once a week, we held a Bible study in the spacious living room. Some of the people who came to us, said they felt that we were almost like family to them. Pouring the oil and wine of Christian love and care into these broken lives through God's Word, became our daily burden.

An excerpt from an article from The Kitchener-Waterloo Record read: "Christians and Christian Churches should do more to serve the poor and the rejected in society," says Erika Kubassek, who opened the house of Zion in Kitchener, May 1984. A large "Christ is the Way," sign, makes clear the purpose of this house.

Kubassek in an interview, said, “I don’t want to speak in criticism, but in love. I think it is our duty to be like the good Samaritan and not shut our eyes to the suffering of people. We must not be Sunday Christians only.” Further she said: “Some of the people are accustomed to a hard-core, tough, anything goes life style, so it takes time for them to learn.” By showing them love, I’m hoping they will see that there is a better way. The Kitchener-Waterloo Record, December 31, 1984.

CHAPTER TWO

Illness and Death's Door

Two years later, I suffered a total burn out, probably because of stress and over exertion. On the evening I became sick, I had a revelation seeing the universe with its millions of glittering stars, and before I closed my eyes to sleep, I heard the Lord say to me, "Trust me." At this time my father was desparately ill in the hospital with liver cancer. Dragging my feet, I went to see my parents in Burlington. This was the last time I saw my father alive. He passed away on December 8, 1985.

My father, a casual Baptist, became very devout in his later years, after suffering many severe illnesses, including the cancer that took his life at the age of 73. My dad and I, although we sometimes disagreed, had a good relationship. I will always remember his words to me: "You must always obey God – no matter what." I have kept this precious advice in my heart since my salvation.

Extremely exhausted and almost unable to walk, I went to bed thinking I had the flu. After some weeks in bed, my condition became worse. Then heart trouble ensued. I went to the hospital for a week, where the doctor said, "I know who you are, I think you are physically burnt out." "It will take a long time for you to get better." He had read about the House of Zion in our local newspaper.

One morning, back at home, my heart raced and suddenly stopped. I will always remember the worst experience of my life – how it feels to die. After my heart stopped, I could feel my circulation slowing down to the point of fainting. At that moment, before I lost consciousness, the most horrible feeling of dread overwhelmed me. In my mind, I cried out to the LORD for help.

Thankfully, the Lord Jesus came to my aid. He started my heart beating again! Immediately, I received a word of prophecy: The LORD is gracious, merciful and kind. I knew that I had heard from Heaven and God had intervened on my behalf, and although weak, it was such a relief to have escaped death's terrifying net. I called upon Jesus and He answered me. The Bible tells us that Jesus defeated sin, sickness, and death upon Calvary's cross and through faith, we are able to obtain these wonderful promises of God.

In Psalm 23:4 we read: "Though I walk through the valley of the shadow of death, I will fear no evil for you are with me." In their hour of death, believers have God's hand to guide them through the valley of the shadow of death and rescue them from the death angel. The unbeliever, on the other hand, dies in agonizing terror – no one comes to his defense when the net of death descends over him.

Death is a spirit, also called the angel of death. He is the last enemy God will vanquish after the restoration of His kingdom. In the meantime, we who believe can say: "O, death where is your sting? Grave, where is your victory?"

This illness was a severe test of my faith. I could not understand what was happening to me. I could only keep looking to the Lord for mercy. For months, I was totally bedridden – unable to bathe or wash my hair. One day my husband, Phil, said, "We have to move from here, since you are unable to get to the bathroom on the second floor." Resisting Phil in the matter, I kept thinking how this would be such a defeat to leave this work of the Lord behind. But, the overwhelming weakness and continuous struggle, proved to be too much to handle. I finally gave in and agreed to move to a nearby apartment building. There my epic struggle continued. Heart trouble and weakness were constant companions. The anxiety at night was almost unbearable. Inside, I felt I was over one hundred years old. By this time I was taking four different medications. My doctor became frustrated with my lack of progress year after year. At one point, he asked Phil, "Do you think she will ever walk again?" Phil and I kept hoping and believing that God would heal me someday. The years went by and I graduated from a wheelchair to a motorized scooter. By now there were only shin bones and some flab left on my legs. I could not walk more than ten steps a day. My legs were perpetually cold, even in the summer.

My doctor recommended exercise in a hot pool. I also tried vitamins, protein supplements, and massage, but nothing worked. The doctor almost gave up treating me. One day, when my faith was very small, I prayed, "Lord, if you want me to serve you in this wheelchair, I will do it." I noticed a few days later, that I had a little more strength to stand up. This was a little sign from Heaven to me that things would eventually get better.

Grief

When my mother was diagnosed with cancer in April 1990, my world almost became unhinged. Feeling like Job, I was approaching the breaking point. The question, "Why," kept coming back. I knew that I was losing my beloved mother and friend: It was only a matter of time. How much time did she have left? Phil and I rented a larger apartment with an extra bathroom, so that my mother could come to stay with us after her radiation treatment. She came to live with us in the fall fall looking wan and pale, hardly able to walk. Although neither one of us could walk now, we were glad to be with each other. I tried to help her in little ways, and somehow we managed for a while. When she became totally disabled, we received some help from Home Care Services. Under no circumstances would I agree to put her into a long term care institution. I knew she was dying, and I needed to spend my time with her; dreading the day she would leave me behind. When water developed on her lungs on Labor Day weekend 1991, we had no choice but to take her to the hospital for treatment. Driving up the hallway on my scooter ahead of her stretcher, I could only say to people we met, "On days like this, you need the Savior." Tears still well up in memory of that black day.

For three months, she and I hung between Heaven and earth. The concept that I was actually prolonging her suffering by not letting her go, didn't occur to me. Her legacy came to me later.

One day when her mind was clear, she said to me, "Soon I'm going to see Jesus and you are coming to God's kingdom too." The phone call from the hospital came on December 4, at four o'clock in the morning. She was gone. In the hour of my greatest need, the Lord did not forsake me, but His promise stood firm. "Underneath are the everlasting arms." He was holding me up with His loving arms. I was able to go on living.

The Healing

Spring of 1992 came with its multitude of spring flowers and brilliant sunshine. One morning in early June, I was driving downtown on my scooter, when I heard melodious singing in the Spanish language, drifting up from Speaker's Corner. I recalled that a group of 'Born Again' Christians met there. As I drove up on my scooter, someone came over and said, "The Pastor, received a message from the Lord, he will heal you today." Getting off my scooter, I knelt down on the pavement, so glad for this message. While the group formed a circle around me and put their hands on me, Pastor Eduardo Riquelme, from the Spanish Church of God, prayed for me.

That afternoon I had the feeling that something had lifted off my shoulders. The next morning, I walked down the long hallway of our building to the elevator. In the mirror at the end of corridor, I saw myself walking, and was amazed how tall I had become. After six and one half years in a wheelchair, I perceived myself as very short, always looking up to people, even though I am 5'5" tall. But, today, I was looking down at most of them. The dependence on the wheelchair and the fear that I could not walk were gone; and even though I had almost nonexistent muscle tone, I kept walking. The glorious miracle had finally happened – I was walking again! The scripture popped into my mind, "They that wait upon the Lord shall renew their strength." Surely the Lord is faithful and keeps His promises.

Now that I was out of that dreadful wheelchair, Phil and I could not stop rejoicing. We thanked God that I was finally walking again. My doctor, the Pastor who received God's message, my family, and many people in Kitchener, were witnesses of my illness and subsequent healing. I was more than happy to give my wheelchair and scooter away.

God's Witnesses

In 1990, still confined to a wheelchair myself, we took the plunge of having a demonstration at Queen's Park in Toronto, on issues of morality. The New Democratic Party under Premier Bob Rae, espousing very liberal laws concerning abortion, homosexuality, and morality on a whole, was in power.

Excerpts from the Kitchener-Waterloo Record read: "Couple from Kitchener organize demonstration.

Excerpt
COUPLE FROM KITCHENER ORGANIZE DEMONSTRATION,
The Kitchener-Waterloo Record, Oct. 22, 1990.

A group of Kitchener Christians is coming to Queen's Park to remind the new NDP government not to neglect Christian values.

Philemon and Erika Kubassek, who founded the Christian outreach group Zion Ministries, are organizing a demonstration about abortion, homosexuality, Sunday shopping, and the environment, among other concerns, Tuesday, in front of Queen's Park.

The group wants to tell the public and the government that it feels Christian values are being increasingly overlooked in policy decisions, Erika Kubassek said. "We're seeing a breakdown in Christian ethics and morals, a breakdown of society, and turmoil in the family. Greed has brought us almost to the brink of environmental disaster," she said. "We want to talk about greed, we want to talk about immorality. We have plenty to say."

Excerpt
CHURCH PROTEST AMAZES QUEEN'S PARK WORKER
K-W Record, Oct. 24, 1990.

A handful of evangelical Christians from Kitchener brought their message to Queen's Park, Tuesday, in a sermon-like protest.

Seven women and two men from various churches in Kitchener, paraded in front of the Legislature, bearing signs reading: "Greed kills creation, immorality is rampant, and God hates sin." They sang hymns, while organizer, Erika Kubassek, spoke out against abortion, homosexuality, violence in the media, Sunday shopping, and environmental degradation.

"I've never seen anything like it, and I've been here eight years," said one Queen's Park worker, adding he was a Baptist. "It's fantastic. Most churches wouldn't have the nerve."

Quoting liberally from the Bible, Kubassek said, "The group had come to show there are still Christians among us."

"We feel this is the best place to speak up on these things because it is the center of the Ontario Government," said Philemon Kubassek, adding they could reach people in Toronto who do not go to church."

Meeting the Premier

The first time Ontario Premier, Bob Rae, and I met, was a complete surprise to both of us. In the late summer of 1991, Prince Charles and Princess Diana, came to Canada on a public relations visit to Toronto. Their marriage was in trouble. After several other engagements, they were scheduled to attend a Sunday service in an Anglican church in downtown Toronto. Planning to give Prince Charles a letter about His 'New Age' practices, we were at a good vantage point, not far from the church entrance.

Positioned in my wheelchair with Phil standing behind me, we watched the crowd. As Mr. Rae approached, I stood up and walked a few steps towards him. Shaking hands with him, I said, "Mr. Rae, my name is Erika Kubassek, we asked you for an appointment, and though you did not want to see us, the Lord so led." While staring at me, his head dramatically jerked back. Without delay, he continued to walk on. We had written Mr. Rae on several occasions concerning abortion, homosexuality, violence, Sunday shopping, and the environment, but our letters remained unanswered. In the fall of 1990, we demonstrated on these issues at Queen's Park. The message the Lord gave us at the time, *"If you harken you will turn away the disaster that is about to incur upon this country."* Then the recession hit Canada with a vengeance. Thousands of people were thrown out of their jobs as companies closed all over. Canada's unemployment rates stood at over eleven percent.

Top Brass

In 1992, the day we met Prime Minister Brian Mulroney is forever etched in my mind. It truly was miraculous. When the words of prophecy, *"Shall I not also go to the kings of the earth?"*, came out of my mouth in 1982, total surprise was on all our faces. None of us, my parents, Pastor Schultz, a friend of my father, another friend, and myself did not comprehend what had fallen from my lips. But, now, exactly ten years later, this prophecy came into fulfillment as I was pushed in front of Brian Mulroney.

Let me explain. During the spring of 1992, we were driving to Toronto to deliver some material on Christian concerns regarding the evident moral decline of Canada to the editor of the Toronto Star, which is the biggest newspaper in Southern Ontario. After leaving the Toronto Star building, located at the foot of Yonge Street, we were ready for lunch. We found a little, but quaint restaurant. Over lunch I suddenly remembered that Prime Minister, Brian Mulroney, was visiting Toronto today.
"Phil," I said, "Would you phone Queen's Park and find out where Mr. Mulroney will be today?" After a couple of minutes, he returned with the answer. "He will be at the Toronto Star in twenty minutes." We quickly finished our lunch, and left in hopes of meeting Mr. Mulroney.

Since he was scheduled to meet with Toronto Star executives, we waited in the reception hall of the Toronto Star office. Among the group of Star employees, was a young woman who chatted with me while waiting for the distinguished guest. Although I was still traveling in the wheelchair, I was able to do a few steps. Then we heard voices, and Mr. Mulroney stepped out of the elevator, walking towards our group. Suddenly, this young woman grabbed my hand, pulled me towards the Prime Minister, pushed me right in front of him and as I landed "smack" barely one foot away from him, she said, "You wanted to speak to the Prime Minister." He looked at me very surprised, but also mildly amused. Introducing myself and while shaking hands with him, I said, "I have been writing to you." Looking at the pale blue folder in my hand, he asked, "Is that for me?" "Yes," I answered, handing him the folder containing our warnings about the moral evils of abortion, homosexuality, and other moral issues. Thanking me as I was saying, "God bless you," he turned to another person who was waiting to greet him. Our mission was accomplished. We realized that this was a divine appointment, a direct leading of the LORD.

Spring of 1993 brought Justice Minister, Kim Campbell to Kitchener's Valhalla Inn, in anticipation of receiving the nomination to become Canada's first woman Prime Minister. After the luncheon, her speech focused on education and training for Canadians in order to make Canada more competitive and productive. In the question period, she answered all different kinds of questions that were directed to her. My question, "Do you support abortion and homosexuality? If so, God will not support you." This brought the admission of her liberal stand on these issues. Kim Campbell replaced Prime Minister Brian Mulroney in 1993 after he had stepped down in 1992.

The first time I actually met Prime Minister, Kim Campbell, was at the 1993 Highland Games in Fergus, Ontario, amid colorful Scottish kilts and the festive sound of bagpipes. After a quick bite of lunch at Shopsy's, we went over to the pavilion. Kim Campbell was in a meeting and would be available to the press later. The reporters had their cameras cocked and ready when the door swung open, and the tiny blond Prime Minister stepped out smiling. After shaking hands with the people, she came towards me. "Mrs. Campbell," I called, introducing myself, "I'm in Christian prophetic ministry." "Glad to meet you," she said, all the while looking a little shocked.

As I handed her the pale mauve envelope, I noticed that her suit jacket was exactly the same shade of mauve. Phil captured that moment on film. The mysterious envelopes I handed out to our political leaders, contained letters and articles, trying to persuade them to stand against the moral sins of our time. But, were they listening? Did they not realize that their actions would bring serious, yes, even devastating repercussions? She turned to shake some more hands and left for the tent, which was set up for her comfort. By this time the heat was oppressive, so we only stayed a short time to watch the event. She went down to a crushing defeat.

Jean Chretien

In his election campaign of October 1993, Mr. Chretien, Liberal Leader, and leader of the Opposition, came to Kitchener's German Club, the Concordia. In the crowded room, the aroma of good German food, wafted in the air. When Mr. Chretien finally arrived, he was thronged. Amazingly, he came right to the spot where I was standing, and while shaking hands with him, I also snapped a quick photo. His campaign speech centered on jobs for Canadians and the economy. Without morals, I would have liked to have told him, there can be no blessings. Those are two issues that are connected, no matter how much politicians wish to sidestep them.

After his speech, Mr. Chretien went out to meet the press. When he was making his way to the bus later, I reminded him, "In our letter to you, Mr. Chretien, we are expressing concern over the moral values in Canada." I received his "Thank You" later, but no changes were made on abortion, homosexuality, and other moral concerns.

Jean Chretien, Leader of the Opposition, went on to become Canada's next Prime Minister.

CHAPTER THREE

Cross-Country Trip

We were then commanded by the LORD to send a message to Canadians with our large air-filled balloon bearing the words, “Canada return to Christian values or you will fail,” and travel across Canada on it’s 125th birthday.

On July 1, 1992, we arrived in Ottawa for Canada’s birthday celebrations. We headed to the Governor General’s residence on Sussex Drive, and as we approached the guard house, along with other arriving guests, we were waved right into the mansion’s grounds. We were thankful that we had dressed properly for the occasion, that morning. Of course, we knew that Her Majesty, Queen Elizabeth, would be there – officiating and speaking on this occasion. The celebrations were already underway. Queen Elizabeth sat under a white canopy shielding her from the hot sun, while next to her was Governor, Ray Hnatyshyn. After delivering a short congratulatory speech, and while the band played, “God Save the Queen,” the Queen proceeded to inspect the ‘Guard of Honor” in their red tunics, while they were standing at attention, on the lush green lawn.

When the ceremonies drew to an end and the Queen was preparing to leave, I rushed forward. Her bodyguard deftly intercepted me. Showing him the flowers and the letter I had for her, in which I was speaking up for Christian morals, he directed me to the Queen’s Lady-In -Waiting. “I will be sure to give these to Her Majesty,” she said. It had been a wonderful day and we joyfully left the Governor General’s mansion.

The next morning, we left for Sault Ste.Marie. In spite of the rain, the *Sault Star* s**ent out their reporters to meet us. On July 6, 1992, the following headline appeared i**n the Sault Star.

"Couple Seeking Return to Christian Values." The article said, "The Kubasseks are concerned about where Canada is heading and are hoping to encourage the citizens of the country to join forces in keeping our nation a "Christian one." They feel that Canada has steadily been drifting away from Biblical principles and is seeing the results as social problems increase. "Canada has lost its unity and prosperity," they said. "They feel Canada has to stop and think. Hollywood is spewing out negative lifestyles and morals are being replaced with the wrong type of thinking. The country is being held together by a thin string, which could break at any time."

Our trek went on to Thunder Bay where the *Chronicle-Journal* featured a photograph of our balloon with the message at picturesque Marina Park on July 7th with the heading "Biblical balloon floated over city." Although Winnipeg sent out a photographer, they did not use the picture. The *Saskatoon Star Phoenix* also did a good article about our tour. We then went on to Calgary, Chilliwack, and Vancouver, sharing our concerns regarding these moral issues. As we drove across Canada, we learned an important lesson about the press and our naivete was soon cured. Liberal newshounds do not welcome Christian comments or views, and disdain, if not outright hatred, is evident.

The larger cities clearly stonewalled us. The Bible tells us that God planned to destroy the great city of Nineveh, but sent the Prophet, Jonah, to warn the people, man and beast put on sackcloth in repentance, and the city was spared. Times have changed. Today, because of the prevalent decadence of society, the major cities ignore Christian messages sent to them. So, sadly, when judgement falls, people are taken by complete surprise – just like New York city on September 11th, 2001.

BIBLICAL BALLOON FLOATED OVER CITY
Chronicle-Journal, Thunder Bay, Ontario

Phil Kubassek and his wife Erika, of the Zion Ministries of Kitchener, Ont., are on a cross Canada trek concerned with the country and it loss of direction. As a result they are flying this special balloon wherever they visit. The 12-foot high balloon, on the back of their camper, symbolizes the country's plight and they hope to create awareness and try to get people to turn around the deterioration of ethics and morals and help bring people back to solid Christian beliefs. They feel it will help put Canadian Society back on the right footing for recovery. They inflated their symbolic balloon at Marina Park, in a brief ceremony before heading on to Winnipeg Monday.

COUPLE SEEKING RETURN TO CHRISTIAN VALUES

The Sault Star, July 6, 1992.

Phil and Erika Kubassek were in Sault Ste. Marie on Saturday to spread their message of faith as they make their way across Canada.

The two are ready for a long trip that includes Thunder Bay, Winnipeg, Vancouver, and Edmonton. They just returned from Ottawa.

They are concerned about where Canada is heading and are hoping to encourage the citizens of the country to join forces in keeping our nation a Christian one.

They feel that Canada has steadily been drifting away from Biblical principles and is seeing the results in increased and serious social problems.

"Canada has forsaken God's laws and lost its unity and prosperity," they said. They feel that Canada has to stop and think. "Hollywood is spewing out negative l**ifestyles and morals are being replaced with the wrong type of thinking," said** Mrs. Kubassek.

The team has been writing letters to provincial Parliaments and has recently met Premier Bob Rae.

They said they received a positive response in Ottawa where they handed out flyers by their huge hot air 'Balloon with a Message,'- "Canada return to Christian values or you will fall."

In Ottawa, they sat near the Queen as she inspected the guards during Canada's Birthday celebrations.

As they make their way across the country, the Zion Ministries hopes to expand in the effort to help others.

Canada's 125th Birthday is an unique opportunity to reassess our values and to affirm our respect for Christian principles and laws," they said.

Abortion – a deadly sin

Growing in each mother's womb is a baby. It's not "a blob of tissue," or a "product of conception." A pre-born baby is fully human from the moment of conception.

Human pregnancy and birth are about a tiny human being with an eternal soul which is forming in the "image of God."

However, in the Western world, every year, millions of pre-born babies are murdered through abortion before they have a chance to see the sun light of this world. They are babies, not parasites.

God Himself, in His own words in the Bible, refers to unborn human babies as, "She was with child," Matthew 11:8, and "The Babe leaped in her womb," Luke 1:41.

Abortion is therefore, murder of unborn babies, which is against God's will.

"Thou shall not kill," is written in the Bible (Exodus 20:13).

According to the LORD'S direction, we proceeded to perform a drama, which I had adapted from the "Diary of an Unborn Child," in various places such as in front of the Kitchener-Waterloo Hospital, Parliament Hill on Canada Day, Queens Park in Toronto, in front of the White House in Washington, and other places.

The following are media excerpts on the subject of abortion.

Ottawa, Canada Day

On July 1st. Canada celebrates its birthday. Every year celebrations are held on Parliament Hill in front of the impressive, old Parliament buildings. Thousands of people attend. This year, 1993, we planned to present our anti-abortion drama up on the hill. When we asked about this occurrence, we were advised to go to Speaker's Corner at the Sparks Street Mall. Our drama, "Here Comes the Judge," adapted from the "Diary of an unborn child," was scheduled for 2:00 P.M. The oppressive heat was bearing down on us as we made our way to Speaker's Corner. A group of bare-chested youths were already in full swing playing their guitars. "Can we put on our play when you take a break?" we asked. They reluctantly agreed. Later, when they took their break, we performed our drama and were encouraged when we heard clapping. However, there were disparaging remarks as well. Most people were silent. We were confronting the silent majority with the abortion issue. The following is the anti-abortion drama, 'Here Comes the Judge', and a media excerpt on the subject.

Here Comes ----the Judge!
Opening Remarks:

The pressure on politicians to abandon established moral and ethical standards is growing and more often than not, moral and ethical standards are left behind in favor of pleasing the permissive segment of society. The government has condoned and promoted abortion by funding it. In the following drama, we would like to draw your attention to the issue of abortion in a spiritual light.

Messenger
There were 1.6 million abortions in the U.S. and over 95,000 in Canada last year. Who has deceived you into murdering the child in your womb? None of your reasons are acceptable. You have spilled innocent blood. Is it not the LORD who gives life? What right did you have to terminate it? The LORD had a great plan for these children, but you have savagely destroyed them.

Messenger to Abortion Doctor
Why have you used the hands the LORD gave you to kill the innocent unborn?

Abortion Doctor Defiantly: I was only helping women so they would have safe abortions and not have to resort to coat hangers. I was doing a good deed.

Messenger to Abortion Doctor
Is not the LORD the Creator of these babies? Who are you to destroy them? Have you not observed all the wonderful creation of God? Have you not noticed how the birds, the animals and the fish great and small live and reproduce? How they work and play? As it is, you have defied the LORD and innocent blood is on your hands.

Unborn child speaks:
October 5 – Today my life began. My parents do not know it yet. I am as small as a seed of an apple, but it is I already. And I am to be a girl. I shall have blond hair and blue eyes. Just about everything is settled though, even the fact that I shall love flowers.

October 19 - Some say that I am not a real person yet, that only my mother exists. But I am a real person, just as a small crumb of bread is yet truly bread. My mother is, and I am.

October 23 - My mouth is just beginning to open now. Just think, in a year or so I shall be laughing and later talking. I know what my first word will be: MAMA.

October 25 – My heart began to beat today all by itself. From now on it shall gently beat for the rest of my life without ever stopping to rest! And after many years it will tire. It will stop, and then I shall die.

November 2 - I am growing a bit every day. My arms and legs are beginning to take shape. But I have to wait a long time yet before those little legs will raise me to my mother's arms, before these little arms will be able to gather flowers and embrace my father.

November 12 - Tiny fingers are beginning to form on my hands. Funny how small they are! I'll be able to stroke my mother's hair with them.

November 20 - It wasn't until today that the doctor told mom that I am living here under her heart. Oh, how happy she must be! Are you happy, mom?

November 25 - My mom and dad are probably thinking about a name for me. But they don't even know that I am a little girl. I want to be called Kathy. I am getting so big already.

December 10 - My hair is growing. It is smooth and bright and shiny. I wonder what kind of hair mom has.

December 13 - I am just about able to see. It is dark around me. When mom brings me into the world it will be full of sunshine and flowers. But what I want more than anything is to see my mom. How do you look, mom?

December 24 - I wonder if mom hears the whispering of my heart? Some children come into the world a little sick. But my heart is strong and healthy. It beats so evenly: tup-tup-tup. You'll have a healthy little daughter, mom.

December 28 – Today my mother killed me.

Diary of an Unborn Child (author unknown)

ABORTION FOES STAGE STREET PLAY TO PROTEST HOSPITAL'S DECISION

K-W Record, June 14, 1993.

Abortion foes staged a play at Speakers' Corner in Kitchener, on Saturday to protest the return of abortion services to K-W Hospital.

The 10-minute play, Here Comes the Judge, was performed three times by Cambridge resident Erika Kubassek and three supporters, including Kubassek's husband, Philemon. "Murdering the unborn is a terrible sin," he said.

K-W Hospital's board of commissioners voted May 27 to start providing abortion services at the hospital this fall.

"We don't feel there's any excuse for abortion," said Erika Kubassek.

Between 10 and 15 people watched each performance of the play, which Kubassek said is based on the 'Diary of an Unborn Child.'

Kubassek and her husband have picketed in front of K-W Hospital in the past to protest abortion services being provided. The region has not had abortion services since April 1992 when a local doctor stopped performing the procedure. Kubassek said she plans to perform the play on Parliament Hill on Canada Day.

The Kubasseks are part of the Zion Ministries, a group they founded in 1982. They travel about Canada and the United States, speaking to politicians about issues such as abortion and homosexuality.

Locally, Kubassek said, the ministry is involved in working with people with physical needs and comforting people without families who are sick or depressed.

CHAPTER FOUR

Visit to Washington

In the spring of 1993, Phil and I were given instruction to travel to Washington and deliver a message in front of the White House for the USA. It was after the inauguration of President Bill Clinton while Prime Minister Brian Mulroney was still in office at Ottawa. He was one of the first world leaders to come calling at the White House.

Armed with our flyers, we stood at the gate in front of the White House, on this breezy, but sunny morning. The flyers read as follows:

> Mr. Clinton do not mock God.
> Woe to America and Canada!
> You have forsaken the laws of the LORD.
> The blood of the aborted unborn is crying to Heaven.
> All manner of violence is found in you.
> Homosexuality and immorality abound.
> Child abuse and incest.
> Your religious leaders have failed.
> Devil worship and heathen practices defile the land.
> Greed and dishonesty prevail.
> Unless you repent, the LORD will
> send unprecedented JUDGMENT!

When Prime Minister Brian Mulroney's black limousine was arriving, and as the Honor Guard stood at attention near the impressive White House portals, both the American and Canadian flags waved snappily in the wind.

While members of the press flocked past us towards the entrance gate, many of them took the flyers we handed out.

Today's liberal media have all but forsaken the laws Western civilization was founded upon – the bedrock of Biblical laws. America, Canada, and the European nations, are slipping further and further away from these Biblical laws, principles and morality, each and every year. Society's morality is crumbling at an ever faster pace; enslaving people to immorality, drugs, selfishness, greed, and finally, violence.

The liberal media deftly shut out Christian commentary, filling the vacuum with lewd, and pornographic content. Christians find themselves increasingly unprotected when they speak out on the thorny moral issues of abortion and homosexuality, free sex, public nudity, prostitution clothed as Escort Services, phone sex, lap dancing, drug and marijuana use. These are condoned by the law.

When God commanded Christians to speak out on these moral issues, He meant it. We are to be a 'salt and a light' to the world around us. Acquiescence with immorality and injustice is an affront to God. But, has the Christian church been faithful in confronting these evils? Or, have they allowed the liberal media and secular world to muzzle them into silence? We cannot, and must not remain silent any longer.

This day in Washington, we confronted the liberal, secular media with a divine message.

With surprise, I noticed a familiar face, Walter Cronkite of ABC TV, who was walking towards the White House. I caught up with him saying: "The LORD gave us a good message." Turning, he said, "I have to rush, I have an appointment." He then disappeared into the White House. Subsequently, our flyer for him was sent directly to him at ABC TV in New York city. Soon I spotted another well known face, Carl Hanlon of Global TV, Toronto, who took time to talk with us and promised to read our flyer. Apparently, our appointments today, were made in Heaven. Many members of the press and the public, took and read our flyers. For this day, our witnessing was accomplished, and we returned to Canada the next day.

By this time, I was writing letters to the local newspapers regularly on these moral matters and was able to publish the occasional article as well. The journalism course I had taken while confined to my wheelchair, came in handy now.

Ottawa: The House of Commons

Though this was not my first visit to Ottawa, it was probably the most pleasant one. The perfectly glorious September weather beckoned myself and two young companions, Nellie and Marg, on our excursion to Ottawa. It was the fall of 1994. We carried a letter protesting Euthanasia (mercy killing), with us. After our arrival on Parliament Hill, I dismissed my friends, sending them off to see the "sights" in Ottawa.

As I strode towards the parliament buildings, I noticed a familiar face in front of me. It was that of Finance Minister, Paul Martin. "Hello," I said, introducing myself to him. "I am with the Woman's Christian Temperance Union, and I'm delivering a letter to the Prime Minister and the Members of Parliament on the subject of Euthanasia." His face spoke volumes! "Thank you," he said. But, perhaps he was thinking, "Here is another one of those pesky Christians, presuming to tell us what to do." As he continued on his way, I rejoiced about the meeting God had arranged for me.

At 2:00 P.M., I attended question period in the House of Commons. When I arrived, the debate was in full swing in a full house, with discussions centered on Canada's unity question, the crushing debt, and the failure of the justice system.

My day ended with a hearty dinner at an Italian restaurant with Nelly and Marg.

The next day, Tuesday, after the session, I had plans to meet Janko Peric, the Liberal Member of Parliament for our city of Cambridge. In the foyer the sign to the scrum area where the politicians meet the press, said, "No access to visitors." Somehow, I had to get a message to Janko Peric that I was here. I then decided to inquire from the security officer in the scrum area where the security is tight, if he could be of assistance to me. After convincing the officer at the Chamber door, that my request was legitimate, I waited for Janko to appear. Finally, smiling, Janko emerged. "Hello, Erika, c'mon," he said, leading me directly into the Members' lounges. Some Members of Parliament stood talking and snacking on plates of cheese, crackers, and fruit. Towards the front, we met up with the Speaker of the House, Mr. Villeneuve. "This is Erika Kubassek of Cambridge," Janko introduced me. "How are you?" the Speaker asked. "Just fine," I replied. "I'm with the Woman's Christian Temperance Union." "Oh, is that the group opposed to alcohol?" he asked. "Indeed," I said. Smiling he added, "I'm not quite in agreement with you on that." "But, life is fragile and alcohol should not be part of it," I answered. He turned to leave and we finished our tour of the Members' Lounge. As I see it: Life should be be handled with care and lots of prayer.

Not at all surprised with his comments, I thought of the carts loaded with alcoholic beverages being pushed up and down the corridors of the "House," by white-coated waiters. Clearly, alcohol is a substantial part of political life here. Are our political leaders "under the influence" when making important decisions affecting all of us? Also, how much misery and havoc was wreaked in people's lives by alcohol? Where are our role models? Returning to the scrum area, I asked Janko, "Is there a better seat available so I can follow the proceedings more closely?" "Sure, meet me here tomorrow at 2:00 P.M.," he said. "Thank you and goodbye for now," I said leaving the scrum area. Curious where I would sit, I could hardly wait until the next day – Wednesday. Arriving too early, it was only 1:00 P.M., but Janko came almost immediately and took me up to the galleries to the front row of the balcony. "This is good," he said, pointing. "Thanks Janko,' I said. I felt that the Lord had given me the best seat in the House. As I bent over, I saw the brass plate on the railing which read: Head of the Diplomatic Corps.

Below me I could see all the Members of Parliament and the debate was on crime. Justice Minister, Allan Rock, stood up to defend the seriously impaired criminal justice system. One House Member stood to read a victim impact statement. There were many questions. "Criminals are literally getting away with murder these days." Strangely, when asked how to make society safer from the criminal element, Mr. Rock responded, "What is safe, is not always lawful." At this point, I was ready to scream, "Let's make laws that keep people safe, Mr. Rock." But, I knew all too well that the security police would have removed me from the Chamber had I not been in control of my impulses.

After the session was over, I again went to the scrum area. On the way down, I picked up my permit to the restricted area from the Sergeant-at-Arms office. Now, I was free to move about almost anywhere. Moments after I had taken up position in the scrum area, Prime Minister, Jean Chretien, brushed past me surrounded by security guards. In a flurry of excitement, the reporters asked questions a few feet from me. Then the Prime Minister swept up the stairs with his entourage in tow. Minutes later, I watched an intense Lucien Bouchard, leader of the Party Quebecois, give his interview, knowing little that Mr. Bouchard would loose his left leg to flesh eating disease, and would shortly come close to death.

"Is this a way to get to these politicians," I thought, "To tell them of God's anger towards Canada. His anger at the shedding of innocent blood in abortion and the immorality of homosexuality that the Canadian government not only tolerates, but encourages by paying for it?" The Word the Lord had given me came to mind:

> *Thus says the Lord God:*
> *I will spread my net over Canada*
> *And the United States*
> *And they shall be brought up in my net.*
> *I will make many people amazed and their rulers afraid.*
> *When I shall brandish my sword before them; and they*
> *Shall tremble at every moment,*
> *Every man for his life,*
> *In the day of their fall.*
> *For thus says the Lord God:*
> *And they shall spoil their pomp*
> *And the multitude shall be destroyed.*

Leaving the scrum area, I was convinced it had been a very eventful afternoon. As we were leaving Parliament Hill walking towards the parking area, I suddenly noticed a man a few feet in front of us. It was Svend Robinson, the gay NDP Member of Parliament, who recently introduced a bill in the House of Commons for doctor assisted suicide. Quickly walking up to him, I called, "Mr. Robinson," and he turned and stopped to wait for me. I introduced myself saying "I'm with the Women's Christian Temperance Union. I'm bringing a letter on euthanasia." Startled, he thanked me for it. Svend Robinson had recently been in the news when Sue Rodriguez, who was ill with Lou Gehrig's disease, committed suicide assisted by an unknown physician. Svend Robinson was present when the doctor administered a lethal dose of medication. Ms. Rodriguez died in his arms. Pondering how this handsome, slim young man with blue eyes could be capable of such rebellion against God, I stood watching him. He quickly put the letter in his brief case and hurried away. Could it be that the Spirit of God put him to flight? I could not stop marvelling how God showed his sovereignty again by bringing Svend Robinson into my path at this time. Copies of our letter to the Prime Minister and other politicians were dropped off at the Parliament Post Office before leaving Ottawa.

Mercy Killing (Euthanasia)

Many people are choosing to sanction doctor-assisted suicide because it appears to be the compassionate thing to do. They say, we put our pets down when they no longer have a good quality of life, so why not people? The alternative, suffering is too unpalatable, but the solution is not doctor-assisted suicide. Rather than encouraging suicide, there should be an emphasis on boosting the sick person's morale keeping them as comfortable as possible, and making them feel loved and wanted. Ultimately, the spiritual dimension can't be ignored. Do we have the right to control the method or time of a person's death? What awaits them on the other side of death's door? When painful, terminal illness ensues, it can be a time of reflection and spiritual preparation.

Excerpt from: Heroes endure and wait for God
By Erika Kubassek
K-W Record, Feb. 22, 1994.

Much publicity has been given to Sue Rodriguez's assisted suicide on February 12. Rodriguez had asked, "Who owns my life?" True heroes are those who don't take matters into their own hands and can wait for God, who owns our life, to come to their rescue. I believe that Erwin Krickhahn of Toronto was one of those. He also suffered from Lou Gehrig's disease, and died of natural causes on February 8. He is, in my opinion, a greater hero than Rodriguez.

I met Krickhahn shortly after he went on television in November 1993. He wanted to commit suicide on TV to draw attention to the issue of assisted suicide for terminally ill patients. Prompted by compassion, I wanted to bring him hope. When I telephoned him and asked to visit, he agreed.

He was almost totally disabled, only barely able to move his arms and hands. I had come to comfort him and to tell him of my miracle healing after six and one half years in a wheelchair. Often, I said to him, "Erwin, with God all things are possible."

We had many discussions on the meaning of life and death, and I urged him not to take his life. "Don't do it," I would say, "God is the giver of life and only He has right to take it." "Suicide," I said, "Is not a leap into oblivion, but a step in front of God's judgment seat." On December 16, we had our fifth and final visit. I went to his apartment, where I was received with Erwin's happy smile. Our conversation in German got to spiritual matters, and Krickhahn admitted that he was not hostile towards God. When our two-hour visit was drawing to a close, I felt urged to pray with him, and he agreed. We prayed the sinner's prayer together for the salvation of his soul.

On the following Tuesday, a Hamilton radio station announced that Krickhahn was taken to hospital with a collapsed lung. He died of natural causes in his apartment on February 8.

I attended Krickhahn's memorial service, where we had the opportunity to meet a right-to-die activist, and tell him about Krickhahn's prayer. He was surprised and probably disappointed.

Krickhahn was a hero because he endured to the end. Taking one's own life defeats God's purpose. In suffering the Lord prepares people for eternal life, if taken in the right way.

Today, February 12, we have just come back from a memorial service for Erwin Krickhahn, who died on February 8, peacefully of natural causes. It seems he was in a coma the last two hours. At the funeral home, the assembled crowd was larger than I had expected.

The man who had been chosen speaker, walked a fine line, never referring to Christ, or even 'the Lord,' but with numerous references to the "hereafter," tried to console the mourners. He gave thanks for the gift of life in general, and Erwin's in particular. Several people offered eulogies, including Sabina, Erwin Krickhahn's daughter. She also expressed the hope to meet him in the Hereafter.

Only one young man, obviously the professional "Die with Dignity" Representative, made a political statement about the "Right-to-Die." This really rubbed me the wrong way. I intercepted him later in the lobby, and told him of the prayer with Erwin and how happy I was that he had not died by his own hand. The young man had no reply to make, he was too surprised, especially when I said, "Remember, God always has the last laugh."

Once this kind of law is passed, it might be too late for the people who are of the 92% of the elderly persons surveyed in old age homes recently, who said they "Feared that they or their spouse might be euthanized."

Our current laws, which are based on the Ten Commandments, should be maintained. Killing should never become an acceptable option in our society.

The danger in legalized doctor-assisted suicide is that it can easily lead to euthanasia, thereby terrorizing the old, sick, and weak. In Holland, that is exactly what is happening.

Dr.Gunning, a visiting Dutch doctor, commented and said: "Once you start accepting that killing may be a solution for one problem, soon you have a hundred problems for which killing may be the solution. You cannot have a little killing. Even if it were possible to have a watertight law, some groups would not be satisfied until they have completely-wide open euthanasia."

Dr. Gunning told the story of an elderly patient in Holland who was afraid to go to the hospital because they might kill her. Her doctor said that he would watch over her, so she went. After treating her for shortness of breath, her doctor went off duty. When he returned the next morning, she was dead. Another doctor had applied euthanasia treatment because he did not want to re-admit her again later. In Holland, they are quite far down the 'slippery slope', and thousands are euthanized without request.

Will Canada, a civilized country, continue to resist the push for doctor-assisted suicide, or will the "survival of the fittest" philosophy return?

We, as a people, will have to choose the right path to follow. Now is the time to make our voices heard on this all-important life and death issue.

Erika and Phil clothed in sackcloth on Parliament Hill, Ottawa.

In front of the United Nations, New York, USA

At the White House, Washington, DC

Erika with WCTU ladies

Meeting Prime Minister Jean Chretien in Ottawa

CHAPTER FIVE

WCTU Connection

I joined the Woman's Christian Temperance Union in the early 1990's, and by the mid-nineties, I was very active for this distinguished Christian woman's group.

This WCTU was founded in 1874. Women like Annie Wittenmyer and Frances Willard, who were both first and second presidents, took up the crusade against alcohol consumption in the United States during the years of the late eighteen hundreds. Closer to home, Bertha Wright and Letitia Youman, were the "movers and shakers" of the WCTU movement in Canada.

American, Frances Willard, in a letter to evangelist, D.L. Moody, whom she worked for one year, wrote: "All my life I have been devoted to the advancement of women in education and opportunity. I firmly believe God has a work for them to do as evangelists, as bearers of Christ's message to the ungospeled, to the prayer meeting, to the church generally and the world at large, such as most people have not dreamed. It is therefore my dearest wish to help break down the barriers of prejudice that keep them silent. I cannot help but think that meetings in which the "brethren" only are called upon are one half as effective, as those where all are freely invited. ('Through Sunshine and Shadow', by Sharon N. Cook, McGill-Queens.)

Becoming involved in a major way, I was asked to accept the offices of Ontario, and later, the Canadian Superintendent of Legislation. My job description with the WCTU included the responsibility to approach federal and provincial politicians regarding resolutions on substance abuse and moral issues – calling press conferences on occasion, and writing letters to the editors on these issues. My work with the WCTU gave me valuable insight and training for approaching the political leaders and press.

On Tuesday, July 4, 1995, we called a press conference at the Toronto WCTU office on the subject of "Lap Dancing." This spacious office was furnished with lovely antiques and old paintings. Over the old, finely carved table, hung a picture of Queen Elizabeth II and Prince Philip. At this conference, about half a dozen reporters directed all kinds of questions to me on the subject of prostitution and lap dancing. Many inquiries were about God and my faith. The reporters were quite sceptical and unbelieving, they sort of laughed at me when I shared my faith with them.

At the conclusion of this conference, I handed out my letter to the gentlemen of the press and it read as follows:

Ontario Woman's Christian Temperance Union
July 4, 1995.
To: The Media

Gentlemen:

It was indeed a very sad day when Judge Gordon Hachborn handed down the sentence that "lap dancing" does not violate community standards," thereby sending the signal to the public that "anything goes."

Stripping, lap dancing, and prostitution are all signs of a degenerated society. Canada is now in an advanced stage of moral decline and we call on the news media to open newspapers, TV and radio lines, so that society can be led back to morality from the brink of disaster. At present, the media is biased against Biblical values and will be responsible as this valueless culture commits moral suicide.

Pornography, degenerate sexuality, all manner of immorality and homosexuality, are the norm today. There is a shocking indifference to the advanced moral decline of our society. History teaches us that unless a society has strict moral laws, it can not survive. Decline and finally the destruction of an amoral society is the inevitable result.

Sincerely,

Erika Kubassek
Superintendent
Legislation

In the evening of July 4th, there appeared a segment on Toronto TV, covering this press conference. The next day there was an article in the Toronto Sun. However, the other papers did not use the story at all. On Tuesday, CHUM Radio of Toronto, taped an interview with me on this subject.

The next morning, July 5th, I had a phone call from the Toronto WCTU office, that CFRB Toronto, the largest radio station, had called and wanted me on the Andy Barry show at 11:00 that morning. Barely having an hour from Cambridge where I reside to be in their studio at Yonge and St.Clair streets, I rushed like mad, in order to get there on time.

The interview on the radio show went very well. Andy Barry said: “You don’t look like someone from the WCTU. I had pictured an old lady with a bun.” Andy Barry, though not a Christian, displayed a very nice personality, which made me feel at ease. He made inquiries from me, and listeners called in with their questions and comments regarding lap dancing in particular. The first caller tried to insult me, but after some rude comments, and getting so entangled in his thoughts, he ended up contradicting himself. Other callers agreed with my view point, and wished me well in our battle. It was quite wonderful how the LORD helped me that morning.

TEETOTALERS TEAR INTO LAP DANCING
Toronto Sun, July 5, 1995.

The venerable Women’s Christian Temperance Union yesterday launched a moral crusade on lap dancing and prostitution.

"Stripping, lap dancing and prostitution are signs of a degenerated society," said Erika Kubassek, the WCTU's superintendent of legislation. "Canada is now in an advanced state of moral decline."

Ban Pornography for good of Society

Many young women, teens and children have lost their lives at the hands of brutal sex killers. They were sexually abused, tortured, and slain by these evil murderers. US serial killer, Ted Bundy, went on record before he was executed and said that pornography ruled his life. If the truth were publicized, it would be revealed that most of these sex killers were motivated by their use of pornography. Why then do we tolerate pornographic videos and magazines to be sold in our stores? All sexually explicit material, strip dancing, lap dancing, and prostitution should be banned out-right. Exposure to videos that depict sexual immorality, such as homosexuality, bestiality, urination, incest, bondage, sadomasochism, child sex with adults, and all violence is harmful. They send wrong messages thereby jeopardizing countless women and children, for financial gain. Our silence keeps the porn business flourishing. Our remaining silence is tantamount to being accomplices to the horrendous crimes against the weaker segment of society. Why is there such a shocking indifference and apathy towards the moral decline in our society? It seems that when ex-Prime Minister Trudeau declared that "the government has no business in the bedrooms of the nation," the flood gates for all manner of immoral behaviour opened. When the ex- Prime Minister and his sidekicks brought in the Charter of Rights and Freedoms; when abortion and homosexuality were decriminalized, Canada's fate was sealed.

Subsequently, film makers and directors succeeded in putting "filth and anarchy" on the screen for public consumption. Pornography, sexual perversion and immorality cause the ruination of human dignity, resulting in disorientation. When the sense of inhibition connected with human sexuality is gone, the conscience is impaired and the integrity of the human soul is lost. The person then descends into further destructive and self-destructive behaviour. As the person goes, so goes the country.

Sodom and Gomorrah had no monopoly on degradation and violence. Our times are comparable – perhaps even worse. The Christian Church is also negatively impacted by this lax morality. Pre-marital sex, infidelity, and divorce are common – and homosexuality has invaded the pulpit. Although the church doors are still open, God's Word is often not taken seriously. The United Church of Canada, for example, and some other mainline churches, allow homosexuality in their pulpits. They have lowered God's moral standards, outlined in the Bible, finding homosexuality now acceptable – thereby profaning God's House. These moral sins don't ever belong in God's House. It's only God's great mercy and patience that they are not already destroyed. All followers of Jesus Christ must vacate their comfort zones, and declare these sins for what they are – u**nacceptable sin.** Disobedience to God's moral laws will inevitably bring divine punishment.

Let's be clear, when all moral barriers come down, the family collapses, and society is in chaos. Hollywood, the film industry, the pornographers, and the media have done untold harm and damage to Western society. They are responsible that the people of today have embraced sodomite morality.

Judge Gordon Hachbron of the Ontario Court, brought down a decision that lap dancing, a form of prostitution, does not violate community standards. What about Bible standards? This type of leadership puts society at grave risk. If the deluge of pornography, lewd, and violent films is not stopped, it will cause the disintegration of family and society. Unless we excise this moral cancer and return to biblical values, we will see the destruction of our country in our life time. Like so many nations that forsook God, western nations won't escape the fate of Sodom and Gomorrah which lie at the bottom of the salty Dead Sea in Israel. "Righteousness exalts a nation, but sin is a disgrace to any nation." (Proverbs 14:34.)

Kitchener-Waterloo Record, March 9, 1996.

Cambridge may tighten rules for body rub parlors and strip clubs.

Bylaw changes going to city council for a vote Monday night would prohibit touching between dancers and patrons at strip clubs and insist that body rub attendants stay clothed when clients are getting a massage. Body rubbers do not fall into the same category as registered massage therapists, who are licensed to practice under provincial law for medically therapeutic purposes.

Operators offer private massage in their studios by attendants who are clothed, partially clothed or nude. Rates go up according to the customer's choice.

The Ontario Women's Christian Temperance Union had hoped Cambridge could revoke body rub licenses issued for three operators in town – one each in the Preston, Hespeler and Galt cores.

"We just couldn't see why the city needs this kind of establishment," said Erika Kubassek, the group's Canadian Superintendent of Legislation. She said body rub parlor operators should find other services to offer in the health and relaxation field. We want business to progress," Kubassek said, but "We don't want the morality of Cambridge to deteriorate further. I don't believe the majority of people favor this sort of thing."

Over the years, along with many hurtful, derogatory comments in the media, which don't merit repeating here, were some letters of support and encouragement to us and to God's honor and glory alone as follows:

Cambridge Times, December 8, 1997.
KUBASSEK considered a Saint

An open letter to Erika Kubassek.

Many of we citizens of Cambridge and surrounding areas have noticed over a period of time, your good articles in local papers.

We are somewhat amazed to say the least, and yes, thankful at the depth and insight and truth of your writings.

That someone is saying it like it is, is good news. You quote lots of Scripture to back up your statements and that is right and proper; for the Bible is as true and relevant today as when first written by holy men of God, being directed by the Holy Spirit.

Of course, some will not agree with you. They may call you a dreamer as they did Joseph of old, but he kept a nation from starving.

Or ridicule you as they did Esther of the Bible, but she saved her people from death by taking a stand.

Or name you a religious fanatic as they did Paul the Apostle, but he gave us much of the Scriptures. Some may say you are too forthright and loud with your voice, but then John The Baptist said, “I am the voice of one crying in the wilderness,” when asked who he was.

We believe you know something of the love and compassion of Jesus our Lord.

May God continue to bless and use you as a great blessing to a host of people. May He give you strength for the day, and rest for the journey.

WHITE RIBBON TIDINGS – WCTU,
Approximately 1995.
What does God expect from us?

What God wanted was not highly trained troops, but OBEDIENCE. The result of Gideon’s obedience.....complete and immediate victory!

Centuries later, Letitia Youmans gained numerous victories in public rallies on the alcohol problem. She too relied on God and told her women followers that she would dare to invade the men’s world – the public platform – ONLY IF THEY PRAYED WHILE SHE DID.

Did you know that we have some present-day champions as well? Mrs. Erika Kubassek recently planned a news conference in Toronto and was later asked to appear on a Toronto radio phone-in show. All callers to the show, except one, were favorable to her stand. Her topic was not alcohol, but the very present concern in our society of lap dancing and prostitution.

The old foes: Alcohol and Gambling

Originally, the WCTU's mandate was to fight the scourge of alcohol. Other issues, concerning the well-being of the family have later been added.

The Case Against Legalized Gambling

1. **Gambling creates no new wealth.** It performs no useful or necessary service. Gambling is parasitic.
2. **Gambling increases welfare costs.** Gambling weakens the stability of family life. Gambling lowers the standard of living and necessitates a larger welfare burden, thus raising taxes. Increased revenue from gambling is offset by larger claims for welfare.
3. **Gambling increases crime**. Gambling always attracts racketeers, underworld hoodlums and strong-armed gangsters. Gambling increases the number of murders, assaults, crimes of violence, etc. The underworld thrives on gambling. Police costs increase.
4. **Gambling produces human desperation.** Gambling victimizes the poor. Gambling leads to embezzlement, bribes, extortion, treason, suicide, and corruption of college and professional athletes. Crime often results from victims trying to recoup gambling losses. Those who can afford it the least, usually gamble the most. Gambling exploits the weakness of individuals. Gambling and poverty go hand in hand. Ghetto residents are hurt the most by expanded gambling. There is no surer way to lose the "war on poverty" than to expand legalized gambling.
5. **Gambling is a sophisticated form of legalized stealing.** In winning, one receives the wages that another person has earned without giving anything in exchange. The larger the winnings, the more someone else has had to lose.
6. **Gambling produces the wrong attitudes toward work.** It promotes the idea that a person can live by his wits and luck without making any contribution to society.
7. **Gambling contradicts social responsibility.** Mature adults try to minimize the risks in life, gambling seeks to maximize

risks. Responsible societies attempt to build security into life, gambling undermines security. Gambling deliberately creates artificial and unnecessary risks. Gambling militates against the highest values of human welfare. History shows that a major increase in gambling has signified the decline of a nation.

8. **Gambling revenue violates all the sound, standard theories of taxation.**
9. **Gambling** revenue is regressive, inequitable, variable and unpredictable. To make public services dependent upon erratic gambling "taxes" is irresponsible. Public service should be soundly financed.
10. **Gambling is socially disintegrating, politically corrupt and morally dangerous.** Gambling is bad business, bad politics and bad morals.

Harvey N. Chinn

Alcohol

It is the government's job to guide and protect its citizens – not to profit from taxes or from alcohol sales which facilitate the destruction of the health and well-being of youth and families.

For society's sake, the use of alcohol should be discouraged. It is wrong for government to make alcohol more available to the public. This sends the wrong message. After all, alcohol is a poison which adversely affects the mind, body, and soul of people – causing accidents and ill health in millions, not to mention the misery it produces in marriages and families. The cost is just too high.

Alcohol can be a killer
The Record, November 13, 1997.

The ancient Babylonians were the first people to brew beer and the Egyptians made the first wine. Today's alcoholic beverages are mass produced and contain between 2 percent and 60 per cent ethyl alcohol. Alcohol acts like a narcotic or depressant drug by poisoning and numbing the brain and nervous system – causing the loss of good judgment. Alcohol is psychologically addicting. It is our No. 1 drug problem.

Drunk driving leaves a terrible trail of death, injury, heartbreak and destruction. In Canada, approximately 1,700 deaths and 114,000 injuries annually result from driving under "the influence" – not to mention the thousands of deaths and illnesses related to alcoholism; the loss of productivity and the insurance claims that result.

After her daughter was killed in a fatal car crash, one mother said: "My 14 year-old daughter is dead. Nothing can ever change that. This man killed my daughter and devastated my family – yet he ended up spending only a few months in jail." Are we indeed letting drunk drivers get away with murder? And are we allowing the alcohol industries, like the tobacco companies, to get away with mass murder?

Billions of dollars are spent on advertising alcoholic beverages – glamorizing their use in magazines, movies, newspapers and on TV as the "in" thing or the "cool" thing to do. Yet the alcohol industries don't show the horrendous scenes of the fatal car crashes or murder scenes which result from drinking their products. Our youth especially are deceived and put in danger by drinking. Some have died of acute alcohol poisoning or have suffocated–apparently unaware of alcohol's potentially deadly effect.

Others are lured by beer drinking and are forever shackled by alcoholism. How many babies are born with fetal alcohol syndrome?

Instead of making booze more available by opening beer and liquor stores on Sundays, government needs to send the message to the people that alcohol is a dangerous drug. More money should be made available to educate the public on the many dangers of drinking and moderation should be the goal, not more consumption.

Government could step on the booze manufacturer's toes by prohibiting the advertising of alcoholic beverages. That would be a good first step in the right direction – and beer festivals, like Oktoberfest, that glamorize a lot of drinking are setting a bad example, should be stopped.

CHAPTER SIX

The Topless Issue

When the story broke that the Ontario Court of Appeal had handed down a ruling declaring that Gwen Jacobs of Guelph was not guilty of an indecent act when she took off her top in 1991 walking down the street, many of us were shocked.

We got a small group together and protested outside of the Ontario Court Building in Kitchener.

Local women protest topless ruling
The Cambridge Reporter, December 28, 1996.

Don't count members of the Woman's Christian Temperance Union among Gwen Jacob's fans

The Cambridge branch of the union held a small but vociferous protest outside a Kitchener courthouse Friday to protest the "frightening" ruling – which makes it legal for women to bare their breasts in public – won recently by Ms. Jacob.

Ms Jacob was convicted of committing an indecent act when she walked topless on a Guelph street in July, 1991. That conviction was overturned two weeks ago by the Ontario Court of Appeal.

Theoretically, the overturning paves the way for legalized, public breast–barings, a freedom the Woman's Christian Temperance Union decries as "insane."

About 14 members of the union, gathered outside the County Court House, held placards bearing such messages as "Sin Causes Death" and "Why Tempt Men?".

"We are here to let this court know that we protest this ruling because it is a terrible thing for society," Mrs. Kubassek said. "We believe some teenage girls will be tempted to go topless, and this will be the beginning of something very bad."

So many women are already being sexually assaulted, abused and exploited, she noted.

"And why?" Because our men do not have control, they do not know how to be modest, they do not realize that sex outside marriage is a sin."

Allowing women to go topless in public will only "increase the temptation" and worsen an already nightmarish situation, she said.

Teenage girls are at special risk, Mrs. Kubassek believes.

Like Ms. Jacob herself, they are "too young and too immature" to understand the implications of their actions, she said.

"They'll be tempted to do it (go topless) for fun, on a dare. And just imagine what will happen then. It's frightening."

Mrs. Kubassek believes most women not only don't want the freedom to go topless, but think the argument of "fairness", (men can go topless but women can't) is a ridiculous one.

"It's like comparing apples and oranges," she said, "A woman's breast is a sexual organ; a man's chest is not."

She said her group is especially upset by the fact that the decision was left up to a single judge. A ruling with potential for such momentous change should have been put to a referendum, Mrs. Kubassek asserts.

Though Friday's protest attracted very little attention – a group of jeering young men were the most noticeable onlookers – Temperance Union members say they achieved their purpose.

"We want to call attention to this terrible ruling. This is just the beginning," Mrs. Kubassek said.

This article appeared in both the Cambridge Reporter, and the Kitchener-Waterloo Record on December 28, 1996.

Cambridge resident, Fatima Pereira-Henson, decided to go swimming topless in early 1997 at the Cambridge Johnson Center Pool. She had requested to use the pool minus her top, because she reasoned if men can go topless, so can she. Suffice it to say, her reasoning was not too sound. Clearly, it's like comparing apples to oranges, in my mind.

As a Christian, I was concerned about decency and morality in our community. Since it was February and very cold outside, I didn't get involved right away, but when women started to telephone me asking what could be done about this, I was ready to move. That started the ball rolling. Because I had spoken out on other moral issues, it seemed like the right thing to do, by calling a press conference. But, above all, I needed to take this matter into prayer and ask the LORD for guidance.

Then I conducted a poll on the streets of Cambridge on February 24, 1997.

Majority of poll oppose topless women
The Record, February 24, 1997.

A majority of women – and some men – said in an informal poll Saturday in Cambridge they did not favor women going topless in public.

Erika Kubassek, who questioned passersby in three locations, recorded 157 opposed, 16 in favor, four undecided and seven who admitted they wouldn't do it themselves but had no objection to women who did.

Kubassek's poll followed an incident Friday when a Cambridge woman, Fatima Pereira Henson, 34, was charged with trespassing when she swam topless for about 30 minutes in the W.G. Johnson Center pool in Hespeler.

Pereira Henson wants the city of Cambridge to do away with a rule requiring women to wear swimsuits with tops at its pools, especially in light of an Ontario appeal court decision that said women have the same right as men to bare their breasts in public.

Kubassek, Canadian Superintendent of Legislation for the Women's Christian Temperance Union, said that while she asked opinions of women because "It's a women's issue," spouses or males accompanying them sometimes added their comments as well.

She said many of them expressed "negative" opinions.

She said she deliberately tried to get opinions of women from all age groups. She said a large number of the younger women were adamantly opposed to exposing their breasts in public.

Reporters flocked to the press conference we called on the subject of topless women.

We simply had to try to wake up the silent majority, so we formed the Moral Support Group. Our aim was to stem the tide of moral decay and toplessness in particular.

Topless swimming offends most people, morality group says
The Record, March 11, 1997.

A fledgling Cambridge group intends to "wake up the giant" – the silent majority – in its fight against women going topless in public.

"The silent majority has to be given a voice, and we're here to give the silent majority a voice," Erika Kubassek, a founder of the Moral Support Movement, told reporters at a news conference Monday night.

Kubassek and her husband, Phil, formed the group after a Cambridge woman, Fatima Pereira Henson, swam topless at a city pool last month.

Pereira Henson staged the Feb. 21 swim before reporters to publicize her challenge of city rules requiring women to wear tops at municipal pools.

She was charged with trespassing after refusing to leave the pool.

Kubassek, who frequently speaks out about moral issues as a member of the Women's Christian Temperance union, said most people oppose Pereira Henson's actions and last year's Ontario Court of Appeal ruling that overturned the conviction of Gwen Jacob.

Accused of indecency

Jacob was fined for committing an indecent act after taking a topless stroll in Guelph on a hot day in 1991.

"Laws have been forced upon us and things have been done to us and we have not had any say," Kubassek told the small gathering at the Preston Scout House.

“It is time we took the power,” she continued, her voice rising “The power belongs to the people, and especially those who walk in ways of righteousness.”

While it only has about 10 members so far, the Moral Support Movement hopes to attract “thousands” of supporters in Cambridge, Kitchener-Waterloo and Guelph in the coming weeks, she said.

While spurred by the topless issue, Kubassek said the group could also tackle pornography, the justice system and youth crime.

“Hollywood has sold us a bill of goods; blindly, the masses, the sheep, have followed,” she said.

“We’re seeing the decline of the family, the decline of family values, and our children are the ones who bear the brunt of it all.”

Donna Friedmann a Cambridge mother of two, attended the news conference Monday after reading about it in the newspaper. She said women like Jacob and Pereira Henson are wrong when they say women’s breasts should be regarded the same way as men’s breasts.

“To me, it’s part of my reproductive system,” Friedmann said. “If men aren’t putting their reproductive system out there, a portion of mine doesn’t belong out there either.”

Topless issue ‘waking up the silent majority’
Cambridge Times, March 12, 1997.

The demand of some women to have the right to go topless in public places now infringes on the right of the majority of women who support maintaining the existing rules of moral conduct and modesty in public places,” Kubassek said. Adding a poll she conducted recently suggest the majority of women are against bearing their breasts in public.”

The Moral Support Movement has started a petition which calls for our judicial and political leaders to reverse the judicial ruling discriminlizing partial nudity of women in public.

“We are very concerned about the well being of families and children and believe partial nudity would bring serious harm to marriages and damage the moral fiber of people and children.

Kubassek said the Moral Support Movement was also formed to speak out against other issues such as adult and child pornography and the criminal justice system.

"It seems that people have left reality behind after so much exposure to Hollywood's smut and to sexually explicit material everywhere. "We are trying to send a wake up call to people," Kubassek said. We fear that families need protection against this insidious attack on the wholesomeness and well being of our community.

Letters to local, provincial and federal politicians were sent.

Ontario Woman's Christian Temperance Union

February 25 1997.

Mayor Jane Brewer And
City Council
Cambridge, Ontario
RE: Topless woman in Public

Dear Mayor Brewer and City Council:

Thank you for upholding community standards!

After speaking to about 185 women in our community on Saturday on the topless issue, it is conclusive that the majority of women oppose toplessness in public places. I have also received favorable phone calls encouraging me to continue to fight for moral standards and offering support.

Most of the women I spoke to were upset and dismayed that Mrs. Pereira Henson is pushing this issue. Many were afraid for their children's well-being! Please be advised that I will be taking the results of my poll to Queen's Park later this week, requesting Attorney General Charles Harnick to do everything in his power to uphold current community standards.

Enclosed are two articles on the issue, one from the KW Record and one from the Cambridge Reporter.

Thank you again for standing with Cambridge women in an effort to uphold morality in Cambridge.

Sincerely,

Copy:
Justice Minister Allan Rock

Erika Kubassek
Canadian Superintendent
Of Legislation

Letter to:

June 23, 1997.

Premier Mike Harris –and -
Attorney General Charles Harnick,
Queen's Park,

Dear Sirs:

Today a delegation of women from the Moral Support Movement is hand-delivering this letter with the request that toplessness of women in public be banned.

Because female breasts are sexually enticing to men, this type of behavior is shameful and totally unacceptable to the majority of women in Ontario.

Toplessness of women in public is NOT an issue of equality – but rather an issue of morality.

Will the Premier and the Attorney General listen to the majority of women and undertake to give direction to the municipalities to ban topless women from publicly displaying their sexual organs (breasts)?

Gentlemen, if you fail to act soon, many women will march on Queen's Park to demand an end to this moral fiasco.

Letter to:

February 21, 1998.

To: G.W. Johnson Pool
To: The Mayor and City Council
To: The Media

Because families and children need protection, we, the Moral Support Movement are lodging a formal complaint on behalf of all decent citizens of Cambridge against semi-nudity at the G.W. Johnson Pool.

It is distressing and appalling that City council did not uphold Section 164 and 165 of the Criminal Code, which forbids public nudity.

Studies done by Kinsey and Masters and Johnson confirm that female breasts are SECONDARY SEXUAL ORGANS.

The Gwen Jacobs ruling only applied to HER case (she was excused because of heat) and this did not eliminate Section 164 and 165 of the Criminal Code. Public nudity (exposing one's sexual organs) is still a crime and we insist that the Criminal Code be upheld.

The choices society makes now will determine it's destiny and if this shameful and perverse trend is not reversed, society will go down the slippery slope to moral anarchy and to disaster. Now toplessness – what next?

S.O.S. – we are sounding the alarm bells and are warning that society is on the verge of moral collapse.

Letter from: Janko Peric, MP/ House of Commons, Ottawa.

7 May 1998.

Erika and Philemon Kubassek
The Moral Support Movement
245 Bishop St. S.,
Cambridge, ON
N3H 5N2.

Dear Erika and Philemon Kubassek:

Thank you very much for your letter outlining your firm convictions in upholding decency and morality in Canada.

I also wish to thank you for adding your voices to those of others in the riding who are opposed to and concerned with the Ontario court decision permitting women to go topless in public. Several constituents have written to me on this issue and have forwarded petitions to my office. Please note that I have in turn presented these petitions to the Parliament of Canada.

Again, I thank you for writing and keeping me informed of your efforts.

Media Attention

Now the media descended upon us – en masse. First Rogers TV and then Jane Hawtin-Live from Toronto, asked me to come on a 'talk show' with Fatima Pereira-Henson. Canada AM did a segment and others followed.

We called a meeting at Kitchener's City Hall and invited the public. They came. The Heritage Room was filled to capacity with standing room only while, others had to be turned away.

How can we go to the beach?
Foes of public toplessness ask
Kitchener Record, June 17, 1997.

This should be a time of going through the garage and routing out the sand toys and air mattresses in preparation for a trip to the beach. But Cathy Hogan-Munroe is facing the summer with a measure of frustration and worry.

And she is not alone. About 125 people – more than 10 times the number who, hours earlier, spoke on hospital reform at a meeting at the Freeport Health Center – crowded into Kitchener City Hall's Heritage Room on Monday night to debate the issue of women going topless in public.

"I'm concerned about going to the beach this year," Hogan-Munroe of Cambridge said in an interview. "I don't want some topless girl playing volleyball next to my son. Breasts are sexual organs. If women want to go topless, then designate an area for them."

This is the first summer since the Ontario Court of Appeal essentially ruled women have as much right as men to go topless, as long as the act isn't intended to be lewd or erotic.

This Kitchener meeting was organized by the Moral Support Group, which opposes the ruling.

"Topless women in public has nothing to do with equality and everything to do with immorality," Erika Kubassek, the group's leader, said as she opened the meeting.

Kubassek advised people to send their views to their MP's and MPPs.

Most people at the meeting condemned women going topless as an act that puts women at risk of sexual attack, forces them to be, as one person said, "judged by their breasts instead of their brains" and victimizes men who are unable to think about breasts as anything but sexual objects.

Some said the issue has thrown their holiday plans into chaos.

"I can't leave my home, because there is nowhere to go," one woman said, "I've been stripped of all protection from the government."

"I don't want to see breasts on the streets," Joel Bennett of Waterloo said in an interview. I came here because I wanted to see what I can do about my choices that are being violated."

Then, CKCO TV did a Town Hall Meeting style show with Diene Verneal.

Topless debate on the air
Cambridge Reporter, June 26, 1997.

Bare breasts are putting Cambridge on the map – again.

This time, the issue has sparked a televised "town hall debate," filmed Wednesday at the Cambridge Center mall.

Close to 200 people crowded the mall's food court to watch or participate in the debate, a production of Kitchener's CKCO TV.

The half-hour segment, entitled Going Topless in Ontario, will air June 29, at 6:30 P.M.

The segment features a panel of guests – including Cambridge activists Fatima Pereira Henson, who supports toplessness, and Erika Kubassek, who opposes it – and plenty of lively audience discussion.

Producer John Matlock said Cambridge was the logical choice of locations for filming since it has become a veritable hotbed of the nakedness debate.

It is also home to some of the strongest opposition to toplessness, most notably in the form of Mrs. Kubassek's Moral Support Movement.

In short, host Diene Verneal said in an interview before filming, the issue is a hot one.

"Regardless of where you stand on this issue, the fact is it's far from settled," Ms. Verneal said. "It's still very controversial, and what we're after today is a sampling of the range of opinions out there."

And that's just what she got.

Audience members of both sexes and all ages got up to have their say, with the vast majority coming down hard against toplessness.

One young woman announced she supports a woman's right to go topless, noting it's a right she exercises regularly.

"If people don't like it, that's their problem," she said. "It's my right."

These comments didn't sit well with a young mother in the crowd.

Cuddling her youngster in her lap she told Ms. Vernile she's dead set against public displays of nudity and resents the "selfish" attitude of those who say it's "her problem."

"I don't want to see (women) walking down the street topless and I don't want my children to see it, either. That's my right," she said angrily.

Most of the men polled also spoke out against toplessness, though with markedly less emotion.

"I guess it's an equality issue, but I'm not sure it's right to push your rights on others when the majority disagrees with you," one young man said.

Another middle-aged man watching from the sidelines remarked that he'd "certainly take a look" at a topless stroller, but added he doesn't approve of it.

"It's stupid," he said, "As a society, we're not ready for this."

Ms. Pereira Henson and Mrs. Kubassek also had an opportunity to repeat their oft- stated stands on the issue.

Ms. Pereira Henson said she doesn't see it as a moral or sexual issue, but as a matter of rights and equality.

Mrs. Kubassek, however, said allowing toplessness will only entice weak men and contribute to society's moral decay.

"We don't even know right from wrong anymore, and the fact that we are pushing to allow women to walk down the street without tops shows that," she said, to a wild burst of applause and cheering.

Also featured on the panel were lawyers T. Sher Singh and Margaret Buist, who support the fight for toplessness, and lawyer Larry Guilbeault and Pastor Dale Hoch, who oppose it.

Other TV and radio shows came fast and furious. Daily I was either talking live or taping some radio show. There was literally wall to wall media coverage from coast to coast in Canada – and into the United States as well. Even Boston Radio called for an interview, as well as the BBC, the British Broadcasting Company. This gave me an excellent opportunity to speak out on the moral decay of our times. TV host, Diene Verneal called me to come on the "Province Wide" talk show, and later, I appeared on the Michael Coren Show from Toronto.

Letter to the Editor
We're Marching
The Record,
February 20 1997.

Regarding the February 11 article, I'll Bare Breasts When I See Fit, Woman Says, the sexual revolution that started in the 1960's has gone mainstream. The results are a dramatic increase in sexual assaults against women and children and unwanted pregnancies ending in abortion – the murder of unborn children.

Youths as young as 12 and 13 years of age are becoming sexual predators.

Now women want the right to go topless in public. Don't they realize that unprecedented sexual assaults, plus possibly murders will be the result of such a ridiculous and immoral stand? Women and children will be the losers big time.

We are "marching towards Gomorrah" if we don't wake up and return to biblical morals.

It is entirely possible that other nations with other religions, where morality is still valued, will destroy the decadent and immoral western world. History has a way of repeating itself, because people don't read the Bible and, therefore, make the same mistakes again.

Topless debate just won't go away
Cambridge Reporter,
March 20, 1997.

The infamous topless debate continues to build steam.

While the issue has innundated local media and even made it to McLean's magazine, the volatile, Cambridge centered debate over whether a woman should be charged for publicly exposing her breasts made it all the way to a Boston radio station last week.

The issue focused on Cambridge after local activist Fatima Pereira Henson took a topless swim Feb. 21 at the W.G.Johnson Centre and was charged with trespassing.

Partly in response to Pereira Henson's actions, the Moral Support Movement was formed in Cambridge two weeks ago to rally the "silent majority" of Canadians against "decaying morals."

They plan to combat the Ontario court ruling which started this favor in December, when an indecent-exposure conviction against Guelph native Gwen Jacob was thrown out, this making it technically legal for a woman to walk in public without a top.

On the heels of the formation of the Moral Support Movement group founder Erika Kubassek is now receiving much media attention.

Last week she gave interview with CBC radio in Toronto, a radio station in Edmonton and surprisingly a station in Boston, Mass., where she verbally sparred with Ms. Pereira Henson on air. "There were a fair amount of fireworks, which could be expected," confirmed Mrs. Kubassek of the debate. "It's such a volatile subject. People feel very strongly one way or the other about it."

Although the movement is only two weeks old, Mrs. Kubassek claims the response she has received has been "very positive." She plans to continue collecting signatures for a petition which she will present to both judiciary and political leaders. Later this week, she hopes to be granted a meeting at Queen's Park with Ontario's Attorney General Charles Harnick to clarify the exact legalities in this issue.

While she couldn't provide exact numbers, Mrs. Kubassek claims support has been strong. Although coming primarily from women, she claims calls from supporters did not represent any age category, nor was it limited to Cambridge residents.

Anti-topless activists from Fergus, Sarnia and Guelph have called offering their help in collecting signatures in their cities.

"A lot of people are interested in doing something in their community," she said. "People can join our movement or just give a signature on this one issue. The time is right for the silent majority to take action and receive a voice ...they need to speak out on issues."

Mrs. Kubassek acknowledges some may perceive this to be an issue of equality, but rejects activism done in the name of feminism.

Anti-topless group going to the Rock,
The Cambridge Reporter,
May 14, 1997.

Today, Mrs. Kubassek will take her crusade to reverse the topless law all the way to the top man.

A delegation from the Moral Support Movement will protest the topless ruling outside Justice Minister Allan Rock's riding office in Etobicoke at 3 p.m. They will also deliver the first installment of thousands of signatures of people who support the topless protest.

Queen's Park
Topless battle rages
The Record, June 24, 1997.
Cambridge group wants ban on bare breast in public

Ontario's topless debate is coming to Queen's Park today, as opponents of bare breasts converge on the legislature to ask Premier Mike Harris to help them keep women covered up.

"We're hoping to draw the premier's ... attention to the fact that women are upset and will be marching on Queen's Park if nothing is done," Erika Kubassek, head of the Cambridge-based Moral Support Movement, said Monday.

"We really think someone has made a mistake in passing this ruling."

The Ontario Court of Appeal ruled last year that bare breasts are illegal only if exposed for commercial purposes.

Since then, a smattering of women across the province have exercised their rights at swimming pools, on beaches, in their yards or walking down the street.

But a recent poll suggests most Ontarians disapprove of women going topless in public.

Sixty-five per cent of those surveyed disapproved, the poll by Angus Reid Group says. Seventeen per cent said they somewhat disapproved and 48 per cent said they strongly objected.

Those who are male, young and educated are more likely to approve of the topless option.

Harris has said he'd like the law to at least limit when women can take off their tops.

But the 25 women in Kubassek's group want an outright ban on women going topless in public.

"Toplessness of women is not an issue of equality – but rather an issue of morality," Kubassek says in a letter she intends to deliver to Harris.

Women demand cover-up action
The Toronto Star, June 25, 1997.

Hot weather brought the steamy issue of toplessness to the front steps of Queen's Park yesterday as women opposed to the idea came to tell the government to do something about it.

Erika Kubassek, head of the Cambridge-based Moral Support Movement, called the legal ruling permitting toplessness in Ontario, "a moral affront,"

Kubassek and her group of about 15 people voiced their worries in the front lobby of the Legislature before marching up to the second floor offices of the Premier Mike Harris, where they delivered a letter demanding action.

Last December, the Ontario Court of Appeal handed down a decision in the case of a 19-year-old university student who bared her breasts on a main street in Guelph in July, 1991.

Gwen Jacobs was convicted of committing an indecent act. She appealed and won, making it legal to go topless providing it is not for commercial purposes.

Attorney-General Charles Harnick said yesterday his department had found no basis to appeal the decision to the Supreme Court of Canada.

Federal Justice Minister Anne McLellan said: "It seems to me that it is an issue that may well be better dealt with by local communities."

Before this, we attended a rally with the KTO (Keep Tops On), in Toronto at the city Hall.

Letter from Jim Brown,
MPP, Queens Park.
August 10/97
Members of KTO and Moral Support Group:
On the occasion of the Rally at Nathan Phillip Square, Toronto.
Dear Members:

I wish to commend you all here today for your commitment to keep decency part of our community. Many of us here at Queen's Park share your view. There are several ways to proceed. Among them: On June the 26th. I introduced a Private Member's Bill to change the Municipal Act to permit municipalities to impose dress codes. This bill passed first reading. As well, several caucus members have circulated petitions urging the Federal Government to change the Criminal Code. We will be reading these in the Legislature for days and weeks to come. Call my office for petitions and keep sending them in.

You have my support. Once again, thank you for your efforts to maintain decency in our communities.

Erika's comments at Nathan Phillip Square, Toronto.

The profanity, the vulgarity the nudity and the immorality that have invaded our living rooms via the TV – as well as the magazines and videos sold have desensitized many people and have robbed many of their sense of modesty and morality.

Now we are faced with the possibility of seeing topless women in our cities parks pools or on the beach. The Toronto Sun recently featured topless women on their front page, as well as inside pages.

Womanhood, the family and decency are under siege! Topless women in public have nothing to do with equality – and everything to do with immorality.

Why would women want to endanger themselves and their young daughters when sexual assault is so prevalent against women and children?

We need a moral compass in these days of moral decay to point us in the right direction! God instituted the family – and when the family is good and strong – our communities are good and strong. – When our communities are good and strong – our nation is good and strong.

A recent poll suggests that the majority don't agree with topless women in public places. The Moral Support Movement will continue to rally support from thousands of our citizens to strongly urge our judicial and political leaders to reverse the recent ruling by the Ontario Court and to uphold Section 174 of the Criminal Code which forbids public nudity.

As a Christian I am very concerned about decency and morality in our communities and urge that traditional family values be upheld – so that the traditional family can survive. Let's remember: When the family fails, the country also fails.

Mayor Brewer and her team sought some legal advice to see if they could withstand a legal challenge to enforce proper dress in Cambridge pools. She and Cambridge city council feared that it would take untold dollars to defend the "Tops-on" requirement. And so, the Cambridge mayor and city council caved in to pressure and sold out, allowing for topless swimming in city pools.

A Letter:

August 18, 1997.

The Moral Support Movement,

I just wanted to say that I am a supporter against women being allowed to go topless anywhere. I believe it is morally wrong and will only cause or lead to other problems. I don't feel its going to make the world a better place.

Now the law says women can go topless anywhere. What will the law allow next!

Sincerely,
Cathy

No top is OK
Cambridge Reporter, October 15, 1997.

The tops-on rule at city pools was washed down the drain by Cambridge council Monday.

A delighted Fatima Pereira Henson hugged her mayoral candidate husband in tears After councilors voted on a minimum attire rule of "a bottom sufficient to cover genital areas for all."

Erika Kubassek with the Moral Support Group expressed her disappointment in council for changing the rule requiring tops. "The decision will be on your shoulders" She told council. "On that day you will remember what I said."

February 5/98

Press Release

The Moral Support Movement of Cambridge, KTO (Keep Tops On) of Toronto and the Coalition Against Toplessness of Windsor are united in their fight against toplessness of women in public.

A petition with 55,000 signatures will be presented by John Nunziata, MP on this subject on Monday, February 9, 1998 in the House of Commons in Ottawa.

Together our groups are challenging the Federal Government to pass a law to uphold decency and morality in our communities.

Topless crusaders turn yellow,
The Toronto Sun
February 22, 1998.

A topless rights group promising a bare-breasted demonstration here yesterday turned camera shy when TV crews showed up to cover the event.

Just one woman from the Topfree Equal Rights Association doffed her top yesterday at the W.G.Johnson swimming pool – the scene of last year's arrest of topless swimmer Fatima Pereira Henson.

"I'm comfortable doing it and it's legal so why not?" said Jeanette Tossouman, 22, of Kitchener, relaxing topless in a whirlpool with other swimmers.

She was the minority, however. Other women on hand for the demonstration kept their tops on when they saw TV cameras poolside and many locals who showed up for an afternoon swim decided against going for a dip altogether.

"It doesn't bother me but, I don't think it's appropriate in public," said Cambridge's Paul Taylor, a father of three. "In your backyard? Fine. But not in a public pool."

"We're usually very busy on Saturdays," Ridge said, gesturing to the dozen-odd swimmers in the pool.

Pool manager Paula Ridge said more than a few other locals shared his sentiments.

"We're usually very busy on Saturdays," Ridge said, gesturing to the dozen-odd swimmers in the pool.

"I think a lot of people have stayed away because of this."

She said one formal complaint was lodged by anti-topless crusader Erika Kubassek when a handful of demonstrators showed up to protest the swimmers' exercise of rights.

Kubassek's complaint, Ridge said, will be forwarded to the city council.

Henson's original topless swim was in defiance of a Cambridge bylaw even though the Ontario Court of Appeal had ruled public toplessness acceptable.

Henson was charged with trespassing and along with Tossounian charged again in July at a second topless demonstration at the pool.

All the charges were dropped last October and Cambridge has since amended its bylaw.

Excerpt of letter from: Justice Minister, Anne McLellan

April 9, 1998.

Dear Ms. Kubassek:

Your letter and enclosure expressing your concerns about the indecent act and public nudity provisions in the *Criminal Code* (sections 173 and 174), following the decision of the Ontario Court of Appeal in Regina v. Jacob has been forwarded to me by the Honourable Herb Gray, Deputy Prime Minister.

As you are aware, the baring of a woman's breasts in public raises a number of very difficult issues, not all of which are legal in nature. On the one hand, it challenges norms deeply held by many Canadians. Public attitudes on toplessness vary not just from province to province, but from community to community, generation to generation, and family to family. However, it also raises issues such as equality. In implications in relation to the *Canadian Charter of Rights and Freedoms,* but also at our beliefs and attitudes toward others and our shared values.

I ask, "What values?" Since the Canadian Charter of Rights and Freedoms was introduced, moral values have increasingly come under fire. Our Judeo-Christian heritage continues to be attacked in the media, the courts, and the political arena.

CHAPTER SEVEN

Obedience to God

God requires that we possess a humble, servant's heart, so that He can speak to and through us. But, He also demands a courageous heart, ready to do exploits for Him. The Bible says: "The wicked flee where no one pursues, but the righteous are as bold as a lion." (Proverbs 28:1.)

He asks: "Who will rise up for me against the evildoers? Or who will stand up for me against the workers of iniquity?" (Psalm 94:16)

Clearly, Jesus invites us to suffer with Him, to be counter-cultural, and not to fear rejection. He challenges us to practice love towards the poor and despised in society.

John, the Baptist would never fit into one of today's churches. He was too rough and his message was too blunt. He wore clothes made from camel's hair and ate locusts and wild honey. What was his challenge? Simply to repent. He had lots of enemies and few friends – but what did he have? Holiness. He was set apart to be the voice of the LORD in the wilderness, calling people to repentance.

Today, like then, God is looking for those who will courageously confront a wicked and sinful generation with Christ's demand of repentance and the message of salvation.

In our case, we were called to speak out on the moral issues of our time and to warn people of God's impending judgment.

A Profile of Erika Kubassek, by Charles Kuepfer, 1998.

At first glance you'd never guess the Cambridge resident is one of the most controversial public figures in Waterloo region.

Erika and her husband, Philemon, live in a quiet condominium complex which provides them with a beautiful view of the

Grand River. The leaves are already boasting their colors of fiery oranges and blushing reds. Within a month the view will be spectacular. It's a view in which she finds beauty and comfort, in the midst of her unpopular image.

Erika's controversial image has been forged by her public protests against homosexuality, abortion, public nudity, and drug use. Yet, her looks are deceiving.

She is well dressed with shoulder-length hair. She looks much younger than her 55 years and her blue eyes sparkle with enthusiasm as she speaks.

Over the past five years Erika's life has changed dramatically. She looks healthy and seems energetic. It's hard to imagine that just a few years ago, she was confined to a wheelchair.

It was back in 1985 that Erika's heart stopped. She had been running a shelter for women in Kitchener with limited resources when she was felled by a heart problem. May be it was the lack of help. May be it was the lack of rest. Probably a bit of both. Erika ended up burning herself out.

"She would give her last dollar to a poor person," said Trudy Kruger, Erika's sister. It seemed like she had spent that last dollar.

The next six and a half years Erika spent in a wheelchair. She tried vitamins, massage, doctor-prescribed pills and diets. Nothing seemed to help her. Yet she had faith that God could heal her.

But things got worse before they got better. Erika was at the end of her rope after her mother died in 1991.

"That was my Job experience," said Erika, referring to a famous biblical character. It was Job whom God allowed Satan to test. He lost his loved ones, his health and all his wealth, yet remained faithful to God. Like Job, Erika refused to give up her hope in God's ability to heal her.

Then in the summer of '92' she encountered a Spanish preacher evangelizing in downtown Kitchener. He had a message for her.

"He said the Lord is going to heal you today," Erika said, tears forming in her eyes and as the emotions of the experience came flooding back.

Within the week, Erika was able to walk a block. She gave away her two wheelchairs, one to the Kitchener-Waterloo Record instructing them to give it to somebody who needed one.

Erika knew that her ability to walk again was a miracle from the Lord. This dramatic change gave her a new reason to live.

"He's given me a new lease on life and now I'm going to do a job for Him," she said.

Erika had already begun to write and send letters to the editors of local newspapers on various issues before she was healed. It started out somewhat insignificantly and rather innocently, but it soon snowballed.

She officially launched her ministry by flying a balloon bearing the slogan "Canada return to Christian morals" from Parliament Hill in Ottawa to the West Coast.

The ministry began to consume more of her time. She began to speak out more on social issues. Once she held a news conference to protest a gay pride parade in Toronto. Unfortunately, only one person showed up. Yet Erika was happy that at least one reporter came and subsequently was given coverage by a Toronto newspaper.

Despite her strong fundamental Christian values, Erika has drawn criticism from within the Christian community.

Rev. John Neu, an Anglican Pastor in Cambridge, said Erika's protests do not portray the compassion Jesus showed.

"Christians should be more forgiving of human frailty," said Neu.

However, Erika is convinced she is doing what God wants her to do, even if it means making more enemies than friends. Even if it means walking alone.

She doesn't have many close friends. Erika is close to her sister, Trudy, even moving from Kitchener to Cambridge to be closer to her after the death of their mother. But Trudy doesn't understand why Erika feels compelled to be the one to take a stand on moral issues.

Nevertheless, Erika is on a mission. She's been dramatically healed and is determined to repay God. Roger Boettcher, an elder at the Bethel Tabernacle in Cambridge where she attends, said that Erika has a courage within her that comes from her heart. It is this courage that gives her the strength to continue on with the mission that God has given her.

Erika's life has changed dramatically. She is thankful to God that she has been given the ability to walk again. She is determined to shake up the Christian community and to take a stand against moral decay within society. She is not discouraged by the criticism she receives for expressing her unpopular views. This is her mission in life. Nothing will stop it.

For now she will continue to fight, knowing someday she will be with the Lord. On that day when she will meet her healer.

Christian History And Apostasy

The Apostle Paul said: "I know that after I have gone, savage wolves will come in among you, not sparing the flock." (Acts 20:29)

The early apostolic Christian church grew and prospered under much persecution from the pagan cultures around them. By 313 AD, Christianity was accepted and people were allowed to practice their faith openly. A new Roman Emperor, Constantine, began to favor Christianity. Even though Constantine did not become a Christian until the end of his life, Christianity became a union of state and religious faith.

In a way, Constantine, instead of Christ, became the head of the church. Gradually, changes were made to the Apostles' faith. Because masses of pagans entered the church, pagan practices, customs and rituals found their way into the early church, and hero worship was substituted for saint worship, and tragically, the church in attempting to meet the need of the barbarians, was itself partially paganized, according to the book "Christianity Through the Centuries (Zondervan). Councils were called and New Testament teachings on many important issues were changed, as follows:

Church democracy (or body ministry) was changed to preacher government.

Baptism was changed from "believers baptism" to infant baptism.

Mariolatry (or worship of Mary) was instituted.

Also, worship of images and statues was encouraged.

The sword and the torch, rather than the Gospel of Christ, were employed. In this time called the 'Dark Ages,' religious liberty was gone, and the New Testament churches were hunted and hounded by the new Catholic church, with the Bishop of Rome - the Pope, as its head, who was supported by state rulers.

The persecutions by the established Roman Catholic Church were hard, cruel and perpetual, leaving a trail of blood with New Testament Christians fleeing into all directions.

Scripture and all writings contrary to Catholic teachings were gathered and burned. Persistent Christian writers and preachers suffered a 'martyr's' death. Further, serious departures from New Testament teaching, included the sale of "Indulgences" to get relatives out of "purgatory." The departure from Christ's teachings of love, was almost complete. In one of the councils, it was decided that Roman priests were never to marry, setting the stage for the horrible moral disasters that would follow. In our time, sexual child abuse is common. Later, the council of Toulouse decreed that the Bible, the Word of God, should be denied to all laymen. Only the priests and higher officials had access to the Bible.

Probably the most cruel and bloody thing brought upon any people in the world's history, was the "Inquisition." Nothing surpasses the barbarity of these courts set up to punish so-called "heresy." By 1245 AD, the Catholic Church was dictating politics of state governments, kings and queens were made or unmade, at her pleasure. But in 1400 AD, the Catholic Church, by its many departures from the New Testament teachings, its cruel laws and reeking of blood of the millions of martyrs, had become obnoxious and repulsive to many of its adherents. In a nutshell, instead of being devout followers of the meek and loving Jesus Christ, the Catholic church had become a habitation of demons. This is when the Reformers came on the scene. Between 1400 AD and 1600 AD, the fires of the Reformation broke out all over Europe.

What was the response of the Catholic Church? It burned many of these Reformers at the stake.

Many thousands fled to the New World because of religious persecution. The Ana-Baptists (Baptists) were especially hard hit because of their biblical stands on these important issues. Foxe's book called "Book of Martyrs", (Martyrs between 1400 AD and 1600 AD), gives a clear picture of the atrocities committed by the Roman Catholic Church.

In the eleventh century Pope Urban II unleashed a savage Catholic army and started a series of crusades to wrest control over Jerusalem and the Holy Land away from the Muslims. In these crusades, rivers of blood flowed – supposedly in the name of God.

The crusades were the popes work, making them the bloodiest religious leaders ever; contrasting with Jesus' love and atoning death on the cross.

Today, almost all memory of the thousand-year war between Catholicism and Islam has been lost, and post-Christian Europe and the Americans now only wanted "peace and prosperity." And yet, the world hears the Arab cry "Jihad" or Holy War in the third millenium all over again. September 11th brought that clearly into focus.

Closer to our time, Pope Pius XII and the Roman Catholic Church remained cruelly indifferent to the pleas of the Jews from Germany, Poland, and Rome itself, to save the Jews from the Holocaust. After all that, today's Catholic Church still maintains they are the only Church that has been entrusted with the fullness of "grace and truth," while continuing to preach a pseudo-gospel. Sadly, many of today's evangelical churches accept Catholicism as "another Christian denomination," - calling them "brothers and sisters." The media reports that the Catholic and Lutheran churches continue their dialogue, and have signed agreements with each other.

Evangelicals and Catholics are working together on certain projects such as World Youth Day in Toronto. Even though Pope John Paul II has apologized for the sins of the Church, he still espouses the false doctrine of the RC Church, which has shown to produce a crop of moral failures, including the physical and sexual abuse of nuns and minors.

A tape of Sister Charlotte's testimony was released in Jamaica during the early 'nineties'. This nun explains how she escaped after 25 years in a cloistered convent telling of the torture, deprivations, physical and sexual abuse of nuns by drunken priests, as well as the murder of babies born of these unholy unions.

After she became a "born-again" believer, for two years she testified in Protestant Churches. Then she disappeared without leaving a trace, and the question remains: Was she killed for her testimony of the truth?

The Vatican denies the physical and sexual abuse of nuns. Until recently, sexual abuse of children was covered up. Now the cat is out of the bag. The US scandals are all over the media and the courts, and they show the colossal moral failure in this church. No surprise here! An aberrant church, devoid of God's truth and Holy Spirit, can't be otherwise.

Timely Topics,
Maranatha News, June 17-July 14, 2000.
Deception Is Rife

When Jesus returns will He find faith on earth? The right faith? Why has evangelicalism lost it's past purity, power and glory in the last forty years? It's largely due to the fact that it embarked on the road of dialogue, intellectualism, and appeasement abandoning a militant Bible stance. Nothing more clearly illustrates the downfall of evangelicalism than it's increasingly close relationship with Roman Catholicism. Roman Catholicism amalgamates Biblical teachings with pagan religions of Asia and Egypt. The apostate Roman church transferred the worship of pagan goddess Astarte to Mary, the mother of Jesus under the title, "Queen of Heaven. Mother of God." This religion has not changed its basic heretical nature at all. It's a shame that evangelicals can't see how Rome's promotion of the heresies of

Mariolatry, their pseudo-gospel, their exaltation of the false "vicar of Christ" – the Pope – makes this religion a spiritually bankrupt church, devoid of God's presence.

Recently Pope Paul, the second, on his trip to the Holy Land, admitted to atrocities committed by the Catholic church. Now let him also admit that their departure from biblical doctrine is wrong. This departure from the true Word of God opened the door of the once Christian church to a spiritual take-over by demonic spirits of a pagan religion, spreading error and masquerading as Christianity.

In 1517, ex-monk Martin Luther of Germany rightly criticized the Catholic church for selling "indulgences" which were supposed to allow those who went to purgatory a faster passage to heaven. This unbiblical teaching of purgatory and the selling of these "indulgences" were meant to fill the coffers of the Catholic church. The sale of these "indulgences" fueled the Protestant Reformation and sparked the horrible persecution, the tortures and killing of many thousands of Europeans by the Catholic church – in contrast with Jesus' love and atoning death on the cross where he paid the penalty in full for all the sins of humanity.

It is essential that we publicly expose falsehood to help purify the Christian church for the coming of the LORD. The Bible says that Jesus will only come for a church without spot or wrinkle. So, let's blow the trumpet in Zion and prepare our hearts and the way of the LORD, so that His Kingdom may come soon.

Christian Week, May 2, 2000.
Standing for God's truth
Letter to Editor, by Erika Kubassek

Re: "Pilgrim pope is pastor to the world" (CW, April 4, 2000). How is it possible that CW (Christian Week paper) praises the Catholic pope?

Surely CW knows that the Catholic faith is unbiblical, i.e. that Mary worship and the veneration of saints amounts to idolatry; that their teachings abound with falsehoods; that the prayers of the pope with other false religious leaders (Buddhists, Muslims, Hindus) are abominable in God's sight.

Until the pope admits that the Catholic faith is wrong, he has no moral authority, he is nothing more than a deceiver. And that is God's truth.

Laodicean Church
Quote

> If I see aright, the cross of popular evangelicalism is not the cross of the New Testament. It is rather a new bright ornament upon the bosom of a self-assured and carnal Christianity...
>
> The old cross slew men; the new cross entertains them. The old cross condemned; the new cross amuses. The old cross destroyed confidence in the flesh; the new cross encourages it...
>
> The flesh, smiling and confident preaches and sings about the cross it points to with carefully staged histrionics – but upon that cross it will not die, and the reproach of the cross it stubbornly refuses to bear.
>
> By A.W. Tozer.

More and more we hear that Protestant churches question the truth of the Bible, saying that many accounts are just allegories, etc. Some of the moral laws, such as premarital sex, abortion, homosexuality, divorce and remarriage, are being questioned, and changes are made to bring these churches "up to date."

Instead of the narrow way Jesus calls his followers to, people seek to make the way broader. Case in point: The United Church of Canada no longer forbids homosexuality, but, shockingly, allows gay ministers in the pulpit. And horror of horrors, there are gay churches now. Recently, the Episcopalian Church in the US voted in a gay bishop. Apparently, some of the Presbyterian churches in the US are likewise buckling under pressure to conform to worldly morality. The Metropolitan Community Church in Toronto is mostly attended by homosexuals who espouse gay marriages.

It boggles the mind that these people don't realize that they are blaspheming God by asking Him to bless these sinful lifestyles and unions. And, where is the fear of God today?

Instead of Christianity impacting the world with the Gospel and Christian morality, it's the worldly morality, or rather immorality, that is creeping in the Christian church, making its ministry an exercise in futility.

Mainline churches are falling down on the job, refusing to obey God on vital laws and commands on issues of morality, and so society at large has no respect for the Christian faith, because no real leadership is given by these so-called Christian churches. The clergy have retreated to the safety behind their church walls, and they now have a fortress mentality that "sees no evil, hears no evil, and confronts no evil." Society, without moral leadership, has abandoned the traditional lifestyle in favour of the "Hollywood" lifestyle of no commitment, free sex and debauchery.

In the late nineties, I phoned into a Toronto radio talk show, hosted by Michael Coren, on the subject of banning the off-broadway show – "The Last Temptation of Christ," because it was a blasphemous play. When I told Michael in my opinion it should be banned, he took issue with me, saying: "Erika, this is not the 17th century," and then rudely cut me off the air. As if God's laws ever change! Blasphemy can never be allowed. Also, in New York, artists made a likeness of Mary, the mother of Jesus, out of dung, and displayed it at an art gallery, dishonouring the mother of the Lord Jesus. Even non-Catholic believers must be appalled at such profanity.

As it stands, many Christians in leadership have failed to be the "Salt of the Earth." The prophetic ministry God gave us to reprove those that are off-course, has not been easy. Many, through fear or pride, would not pay heed to our warnings. Yet, we have to carry out what God has commanded us to do, and let the chips fall where they may.

Let's be candid, God's Holy Spirit can't abide in a sinful, morally corrupt church. Today's pseudo-Christian churches, masquerading as Christianity, have absolutely no resemblance to the holy early church, founded by Jesus Christ, His Apostles, and prophets of the New Testament.

As we enter the third millenium, we can hear the thundering hooves of the Horsemen of the Apocalypse. Once again, God is speaking to a fallen humanity. We need men and women who are ready and willing to step forward to declare God's message of repentance and salvation to a world gone awry – to let them know that sexual immorality, abortion, New Age demon worship, greed and cruelty, will shortly bring God's final judgment.

Ministers, God's messengers, must be unafraid to admonish a wicked world was well as encourage the remnant of God's children to persevere and to adhere to God's Word. To love and forgive one another, even their enemies, and above all they obey, honour and worship, the Lord our God. Then, and only then, can they have that blessed assurance that God's security system will not fail them even as the world descends into untold chaos, because underneath God's children are the everlasting arms of God. (Deut. 33:27).

Politicians

The major problem in the Western world is that real Christian laws and principles have been largely left behind, and even if a President or Prime Minister belongs to a church, he for some reason won't or can't set the Christian example.

Canadian Prime Minister Jean Chretien or US ex-president, Bill Clinton, are prime examples of moral inertia and moral failure, promoting a godless agenda.

In 1999, I had a chance to attend a press conference in Ottawa with both Prime Minister Jean Chretien, and the former, US President, Bill Clinton.

Maranatha News, Toronto,
November 1999.
President Clinton's Ottawa Visit

Recently, American President Bill Clinton descended on Air Force One into Ottawa, to open the new American Embassy, and later to attend the International Conference on federalism, at Mont Tremblant in Quebec.

At a press conference held at the Parliament building in Ottawa, the U.S. and Canadian media peppered the U.S. President with a variety of questions. Prime Minister Jean Chretien was also present. Clinton's main focus was the ratification of the comprehensive Test Ban Treaty, which is supposed to ban testing of nuclear weapons world-wide. It has since become clear that Mr. Clinton lost his bid to ban tests and that the world has become a more dangerous place.

Further, President Clinton mentioned that even though there have been many stunning technological and bio-technological advances, the deepest problem is human nature. Religious fights and fear of the "the other" is the cause of many of our troubles and wars.

The failure to quickly ratify the nuclear test ban treaty means that rogue states and terrorist groups might test nuclear devices that can't be detected and might explode them in American or European cities.

I also had a question for the President. After several unsuccessful attempts I sent a quick prayer to heaven for help. Lord, help me to get my question in before the press conference is over, I prayed. Finally, I got my chance to address the President:
"President Clinton, I said, there have been a lot of natural disasters lately. Don't you think that God is speaking from heaven because of the moral decay, the abortions and the violence? Have you thought about that?" "Yes," he answered, "I have thought about that." There has been an increase of natural disasters, both in frequency and intensity and I also know that many people are concerned about the millennium – but I think we are doing it to ourselves, referring to global warming.

He is right only in the sense that humanity is doing it to themselves because of their collective sin. Scientists blame global warming caused by burning fossil fuels for the many natural catastrophes. However, we have to look deeper here. In the last three years rainforests went dry and deserts flooded. Stifling heat waves and droughts led to wildfires and crop failures. Hurricanes, tornadoes, floods mudslides caused further damage including loss of human and animal life. The plagues of insects, rodents and snakes are making life miserable in many places. There were outbreaks of debilitating diseases like malaria, encephalitis, hantavirus, Lyme disease, West Nile virus, SARS, and Mad Cow disease. The smoke from many forest fires made breathing difficult for man and beast. And that is not all, major earthquakes can be added to the list of woes. What or who is behind these climatic changes and disasters? The apocalyptic book of Revelation reveals God's increasing punishment of the world's population for their sinful practices and wicked behavior, culminating with Armageddon, the Day of the Lord. Western civilization is in possession of God's law book, the Bible, bought with the blood of many martyrs – but has cast away the counsel of the Lord by ignoring His Word and His laws. So-called Christianity is changing the Gospel of Jesus and the Word of God, creating their own brand of a compromising all-inclusive world religion. No wonder God is frowning and judgment is falling.

Unmistakably, God is speaking again from heaven, as He did in the days of Noah, with many signs and warnings. His holy character has not changed. But are the leaders and the people listening?

In May of 2003, I attended the "Hidden Pierre Trudeau" conference at the University of Waterloo. After the opening remarks about Mr. Trudeau's faith and tenure as Prime Minister of Canada, I stood at the microphone, available for questions and comments, voicing my opinion on Mr. Trudeau's political record, as well as his religion.

In the opening remarks, some speakers claimed that Pierre Trudeau was a "spiritual" person – that his politics were guided by his religious convictions. Indeed? He was instrumental in making divorce easier to obtain, in decriminalizing abortion and homosexuality.

It's the height of hypocrisy to say that he was a "Christian." But, apparently, as a Catholic, he and other political leaders justify holding "private and public views" on matters of morality – keeping them compartmentalized so as not to offend the public. How convenient. It's just NOT what Jesus Christ, the Apostles and Prophets taught.

After the morning session, as I was walking to the dining room, I met up with former Prime Minister, John Turner. (He very briefly held office after Pierre Trudeau left.) After introducing myself and shaking hands with him, I said: "Mr. Turner, I just finished a book called 'One Moment to Midnight', - the LORD will bring judgment because of the collapse of morality in the whole Western world." He responded with shock and surprise. I walked away, knowing that another "King of the World," had heard from God.

Later, in his keynote luncheon address, Mr. Turner defended Mr. Trudeau's and his own actions in changing Canada's laws, thereby removing the protection of morality in the land.

In his address, Mr. MacEachen, one of the other speakers, said: "Voters may not have realized that Trudeau was a committed Roman Catholic, but Sunday mass was a must for Pierre Trudeau." "And further, although Trudeau's cabinet included many Roman Catholics, he said that they kept their faith hidden as a matter of prudence." How convenient!

So, clearly, Trudeau and his cabinet bear a lot of responsibility in Canada for today's moral decline. Divorce is rampant, abortion is wide-open, so that a baby can be aborted up to the time of birth. To date, there is no abortion law in Canada because our legislators could not agree on one. Gays not only practice homosexuality, they have 'spousal rights' given to them, and under the law, have the status of a common law couple. Now they demand to be "married," – and are doing so in Ontario and British Columbia; thanks to our social activists judiciary.

All this was possible because Trudeau opened the door, and other politicians followed, pretending to be "Christians." In the meantime, they were, and are more like the devil's disciples instead of Christ's. Clearly, Catholicism is NOT the Christianity Jesus and his followers preached. It's a counterfeit religion.

Ottawa Protest

Later, a small group of Christians accompanied us to Ottawa, where we protested on the subjects of child pornography, homosexuality, and the removal of the Christian prayer from schools. We are in a national emergency!

Where the hand of the Lord and Pay stubs meet, National Post, October 19, 1999.

Well, we can't say we weren't warned. Halfway through Question Period yesterday, a woman in the visitors' gallery (Erika Kubassek) threw a few dozen sheets of orange paper onto the Commons floor. The woman was quickly escorted from the House by security guards, as pamphleteers and other causers of commotion generally are.

The sheets bore an urgent message from The Moral Support Group in Cambridge, Ontario. It read: "Now, the Liberal Government is unmasked!" Eager opposition MPs, reading on, found three articles of indictment against the current government:

"l. They Don't Protect Children." This is because the government is letting the courts ponder child pornography, rather than overriding constitutional rights to jail people in possession of child porn.

"2. They are Changing 58 Laws declaring homosexuals "spouses" for the purposes of receiving spousal benefits and so on." THE LIBERAL PARTY IS ANTI-FAMILY AND ANTI-DECENCY.'

"3. They are Removing Christian Prayer." Here fewer specifics were offered, but the conclusion was sweeping. 'THEY ARE ANTI-CHRIST.'

"THEREFORE," the pamphlet concluded, 'LET IT BE KNOWN THAT THE LORD WILL REMOVE HIS HAND OF PROTECTION FROM THIS INCREASINGLY GODLESS NATION."

I'm trying to figure out why nobody told us about this earlier. Here I thought the big problems were high taxes and the brain drain, and nowhere is this stuff about the hand of the Lord. Surely a hand-of-the-Lord drain is worse than a brain drain.

I also wondered whether it was significant that most of the pamphlets fell on the Progressive Conservative caucus. Did the woman think the Tories constitute Canada's only hope of salvation?

In conclusion, we can see that the last days will be characterized by apostasy and a refusal to endure sound doctrine, like the early church of Laodicea (Rev. 3:14).

Will Jesus Find faith on the earth when He returns?

CHAPTER EIGHT

World Religions

In August 2000, the Millenium Peace Summit of religious leaders, took place in New York City. Here, at the United Nations, many leaders of world religions met to discuss ways to achieve peace between these various religions.

The religions that participated were:

Christianity (Catholic, Lutheran, Presbyterian, and Baptist), Islam, Judaism, Shinto, Buddhism, Hindu, Bahai, Sikhism, Indigenous, Zoroastrian, and Native religions.

Opening remarks by Bawa Jain
THE RELIGIOUS DIMENSION IN THE WORK OF THE UNITED NATIONS
August 28, 2000, The United Nations General Assembly Hall.

Your Holinesses, Your Excellencies, ladies and gentlemen, welcome to the opening ceremonies of the Millennium World Peace Summit of Religious and Spiritual Leaders.

It is a great honor and joy for me to greet you as we embark on the important task that has brought us together.

For over two years I have been traveling to nearly every region of the world, to consult with many of you on the purpose and goals of the World Peace Summit. I have sought your blessings for this initiative to join spiritual and political efforts in the quest for global peace and security. It is your blessings, I believe, that have brought us to this day, that have enabled you to gather, representing the spiritual leadership of the human family, in this great hall the United Nations General Assembly Hall.

This Hall has witnessed many debates and dialogues among nations large and small. It is here that issues most critical to the human community are addressed by the world's political leadership. One week from today the heads of state of all UN member nations will gather in this same Hall, to address some of the same issues that you will deliberate over during the next several days. It is the goal of this Summit to send a strong message of commitment to those heads of state who will gather, to work with them for the transformation of conflict into peaceful co-existence; for the healing of past injuries; for the formation of a new culture of acceptance and respect for all, and for a renewed commitment to the spiritual values that form the basis of all the great religious traditions.

There are enormous challenges facing us the human community. Dozens of violent conflicts are taking place in the world today. Many of the world's people continue to live in dire poverty. The health of our environment is threatened as never before. I do not believe these crises can be solved without your leadership, wisdom, guidance, and blessings. The world will be watching over the next few days for the voice of their spiritual leaders. The question has been asked: "What can we, realistically, hope to accomplish in these few days?"

Just your gathering in this Hall carries great significance. Just your coming together from so many distant regions shows a unity of intention that can have far reaching results.

This afternoon, this General Assembly Hall will become a Sanctuary, where the prayers and blessings of you, our esteemed religious leaders, will permeate these walls and leave their imprint for years to come. This is truly an historic occasion, and fitting for the beginning of a new Millennium. Never before have the world's religious leadership gathered at the United Nations in this Hall to give their blessings and support to the enormous and challenging undertakings of this vital institution.

Increasingly, matters of war and peace rest here. What better place for the world's religious leadership to gather to give their blessings than in the Hall where so many of the world's conflicts must be addressed; where nations must come together to seek to redress the unacceptable conditions of poverty that plague the human community; and where new commitments to preserve and restore our planet must be made for the sake of future generations.

Let us come together for this World Peace Summit in a spirit of unity, putting aside the many billions of people who follow our faith traditions. I believe our combined theological and political differences, that we may send a powerful message of peace to efforts have the potential to set a new course for peace. In the process of putting together this Summit, many obstacles were encountered and surmounted, and I realized there was higher purpose, a Divine purpose, in bringing to the United Nations the spiritual resources of the human family.

This afternoon we will share prayers, invocations and meditations for peace from many of the faith traditions. Before the evening is over, I ask each one of you, to leave within this Assembly Hall your blessings for the work and success of this important institution the United Nations your blessings for the initiatives that will grow out of this World Peace Summit, and your blessings for the future of humanity.

Meeting World Religious Leaders

The following day I had the opportunity to attend some of the meetings held at the Waldorf Astoria Hotel in New York. As a columnist for Maranatha News (Toronto), I intended to interview some people and write an article.

Because many deaths, injuries, imprisonment and enslavement result from clashes between world religions, the question was raised: "Why is there no real peace between religions?" All major religions have gone to war with one another. Catholics and Orthodox Christians killed Muslims, millions of Christians died in the two world wars by killing each other. For years Catholics and Protestants fought and killed each other in Northern Ireland, Muslims went to war with Jews, and vice versa. Muslims fought Hindus. Muslims attacked Muslims. Over two million Christians died in the Sudan, as well as other parts of the world, at the hands of militant Muslims.

The current conflict in the Middle East between Muslims and Jews is the top news story in the world today. The Palestinian people declared an "Intifada", or struggle for independence against Israel. As Jews and Muslims battle fiercely, many are killed. Suicide bombers target Israeli citizens on a regular basis. Why?

It is a struggle about the Holy Land, Israel, and the difference in their religion.. Until 70 AD, the Jewish Temple stood upon the temple mount in the midst of Jerusalem, where two Muslim Mosques are today. This holy site is part of the reason for much contention between Muslims and Jews. Both sides claim the Holy Land as theirs, and both claim sovereignty over Jerusalem and other holy sites. The Jews want the right to live in the modern state of Israel, which was founded in 1948 when the Jews returned to their homeland from the Diaspora, which was promised to them by God, in the Holy Scriptures. Prophecy came into fulfillment here.

With all the bloodshed that is done in the name of God, the real question of course, should be: What kind of god are they serving anyway? The God of the Bible commands: "You shall not kill." There can be no holiness without love. Where hatred rules, God is absent. Often the real motives for violence are political, economic or ethnic in nature.

At the Waldorf Astoria, I had a great opportunity to ask leaders of different religions, about the persecution of Christian missionaries and Christian believers in their countries. Though the Western liberal media ignores the fact that there are thousands imprisoned, enslaved, maimed and murdered by Muslims and Hindus, this news must come out and be made known in the civilized world.

When I questioned some Muslim leaders about these matters, their reaction was peculiar indeed. Conversing with one leader, while the others nodded in agreement, he said, "Christianity can be compared to the human body. When it is sick you must cut the diseased body part off." It is a known fact and has been reported in the Christian media, that the cruelty in some Muslim countries towards Christians and even their own people, is beyond measure. In Sudan for instance, 2 million Christians were killed and many maimed or forced to convert to Islam – not sparing even very young children hacking off their limbs. Women in Islamic countries are systematically oppressed and there are "honor killings" performed. Another torture perpetrated upon some young Muslim girls, is female circumcision.

The war cry: "The world for Islam," forebodes cruel and enslaving tactics.

There is no doubt in my mind that this cruel religion, I believe, is birthed by demons and devils, and that Mohammed was a false prophet. How do I know? This false prophet has brought death and destruction upon millions of innocent people – a far cry from our loving Savior Jesus, who said: BY THEIR FRUITS YOU SHALL KNOW THEM.

Some courageous Christian leaders, namely Pat Robertson and Franklin Graham, have clearly responded to President Bush's claim that Islam is a peaceful religion. They said that this was simply not true. Apparently, the Koran says that Muslims are to "go kill the infidels." History proves that Islam is a violent, cruel religion.

The Hindu response to my question about the persecution of Christians in their country was that they had a fear that Christian missionaries would be a threat to their culture. The question arises: Do they fear that Christianity would liberate the people from the oppressive caste system? Their spiritual leaders were mostly astrologers, and I witnessed to them about Jesus. I then moved on to ask a Jewish man the same question. He admitted that more needs to be done to alleviate religious violence. My plea to God on behalf of Israel, is that He remove the "veil of Moses" from Jewish eyes, so that they recognize Jesus, their Messiah. This "veil" can only be removed by much prayer and suffering. At this time in history, the Jews are going through what is called, prophetically, "Jacob's Trouble." Now, more than ever, we are reminded to pray for the peace of Jerusalem and the Jewish people, so they can be redeemed.

On the surface, the call at the World Peace Summit for tolerance and compromise, sounds good. However, true followers of Christ have the mandate to "go into all the world and preach

Christ's message of salvation." They can't compromise with other religions just to have peace. Christ gave the mandate and the authority to teach God's truth to the adherents of all other religions.

I was thankful to God for giving me the opportunity to meet and witness to quite a few religious leaders. Among them was the Muslim Grand Mufti of Yugoslavia, the Catholic Bishop of Beijing, the spiritual leader of Bangladesh, who is a descendant of Mohammed and various others.

The only way out of the dilemma of religious violence in the Middle East and in the rest of the world, to make an end to the hatred, the bloodshed, and all violence, is by accepting the invitation of the "Prince of Peace," Jesus Christ and obeying His words of love contained in the Holy Bible. As the old Testament prophet foretold, "Then they will beat their swords into plowshares and their spears into pruning hooks. Nation will not take up sword against nation, nor will they train for war anymore," (Isaiah 2:4)

The question then why religions can't get along peaceably, has one answer: Most world religions, other than Judaism and biblical Christianity, originate from demonic spirits and are false religions. God's Holy Spirit won't compromise with demonic religions. Murder and strife is the result of the demonic influences of these false religions. God's Holy Spirit gives peace and the lamb-like followers of Jesus, suffer the persecution of these misguided adherents of false religions. We note that instead of peace, the LORD sent the sword on September 11, 2001, and peace was taken from the earth. Sadly, since then, many have died as a result of war in different parts of the world, so that the Millennium World Peace Summit was actually an exercise in futility.

New Age Religion
The Cambridge Reporter
May 23, 1998.

We are bombarded with images of stars, moons and suns everywhere we go. They appear in stores, restaurants, on decorations and clothing. And, shockingly, we come face to face with hideous winged, horned plaster demons. The plaster face of Satan himself stares from the walls of art or gift stores. These are the emblems of the New Age.

Unfortunately many people are apparently unaware of the master mind behind the New Age movement and they buy unto this deceptive religion

By banishing Christian truth and values from the screen, Hollywood has opened the way for deadly, counterfeit messages. The trend on TV and in movies is to portray evil as good and good as evil. Morality as boring and evil as delightful. New age practices like channeling, visualization and crystal therapy flourish; and New Age terms like higher consciousness, centering global village, holistic and harmonic convergence are commonplace. Through politics, medicine, ecology, education, psychology, nutrition, entertainment, business and science the New Age movement has heavily influenced the Western world.

It has entered into our schools and universities, our professions, business, the media and the political arena. We are presented with a counterfeit religion, counterfeit values and a counterfeit world system.

The New Age quest, of course, is to replace Christianity with another spirituality. The important question here is "what spirits?" The New Age movement is not new. It is really the age-old path of Eastern mysticism, traceable to the ancient Egyptian, Babylonian and Chaldean religions. This "new" religion is attracting adherents by the millions. The New Age "spiritual guides" are actually the recycled spirits of Paganism and Occultism in disguise. Hence the new craze is for statues and pictures of demons, devils, wizards, and witches.

Since the New Age religion and Christianity are diametrically opposed to each other, none of the New Age practices or emblems belong in Christian churches, homes, or lives.

The ascent of the New Age religion goes back to the 1960's and the sexual revolution. Sexual immorality and drug use opened the door to demonic forces and now, some forty years later, we see the result of the rebellious 60's and 70's. Leading New Agers have written, produced art and music so that we see a very changed world before our very eyes.

The Bible says: The Spirit explicitly says that in later times some will fall away from the faith, paying attention to deceitful spirits and doctrines of devils. 1.Tim. 4:1.

High profile personalities such as the Beatles and Shirley Maclaine, among many others, helped to popularize New Age thinking and have influenced many millions.

Harmful occult practices like visiting fortune tellers, believing in horoscopes and a smorgasbord of spiritual substitutes for Christianity, are commonplace. Tragically, the western world forsook its Christian roots and is caught up in the New Age religion.

In the last while, Harry Potter books have become very sought after reading material. Millions of books have hit the book shelves. Young and old are delving into these sinister occult books. They don't realize that dabbling in the occult inevitably causes demonic possession and ultimately puts them on the path to hell. Because the proponents of the New World Order feel threatened by the Christian world view, they do their utmost to muffle biblical expression in the media.

Tragically, these New Agers are sowing to the wind and will eventually reap the whirlwind of God's wrath.

And finally, the deceptive view that "all roads lead to Rome and all religions lead to God," is, of course erroneous. The Bible teaches us that many "false prophets" have gone out into the world to deceive many people. (1 John 4:1)

Jesus said: "I am the light of the world" and also "No one comes to the Father, but by Me." (John 8:12 and John 14:6).

We need to recognize that it is only through Christ's atoning sacrifice can man, woman, or young person receive forgiveness and spiritual re-birth necessary to have eternal life with God.

Pot Use

Along with sexual immorality and occult practices, drug use, such as smoking marijuana, is part of the New Age lifestyle. Proponents of pot use now push for the legalization of the noxious weed.

New Agers, belonging to the "Church of the Universe," such as Michael Baldassaro and Walter Tucker, proclaim that cannabis is a "comfort of God." In August of 1999, they officially opened the second Cannabis Carnival by lighting a marijuana cigarette in Victoria Park in Kitchener.

Letter from Martin Cauchon,
Minister of Justice and Attorney General of Canada.
April 29, 2003.

Thank you for your correspondence of December 13, 2002, concerning reforms to the possession of cannabis offence.

As you may be aware, the House of Commons Special Committee on the Non-Medical Use of Drugs tabled its report on December 12, 2002, and recommended that the offence of possession of cannabis remain with the *Criminal Code.* However, the report also suggested that the Ministers of Justice and Health establish a comprehensive strategy for decriminalizing the possession and cultivation of 30 g or less of cannabis for personal use.

In addition, the Senate Special Committee on Illegal Drugs released its report in September 2002. The report recommended that an exemption scheme be adopted in the *Controlled Drugs and Substances Act* for the production and sale of cannabis. In effect, this recommendation would legalize the possession of cannabis, regardless of the amounts involved.

The Government is currently considering both reports before taking a final position on the question of reforms to the possession offence. I would add that no consideration is being given to legalizing the use of marijuana for recreational purposes.

Any drug policy must be developed within the broad context of health and social policies, federal mandates, and a collective will of the people of Canada. This is the responsible approach, and it is the approach we will follow.

Thank you again for taking the time to share your views.

Yours Sincerely,

Martin Cauchon

Recent media reports, however, show that there is support for the decriminalization of pot possession, opening the door for more pot use by the public. Escaping reality through the recreational use of drugs, shows that society is losing its grip and is sliding down the 'slippery slope' to demonic enslavement and possession. Increased mental illness, social problems, accidents, and violence are the sad result.

Pot party draws proponents, protesters, police
The Record, August 16, 1999.

A sweet-smelling cloud hung over Kitchener's Victoria Park, Saturday, as cannabis fans gathered to celebrate their sacred weed.

"What we're trying to do today is to educate people about all the positive uses of cannabis," said Davin Charney, one of the organizers of the second annual Cannabis Carnival.

It was hard to tell how many people were at the carnival, which centered on the clock tower, and how many were just out for a sunny afternoon in the Park. At peak, the event seemed to attract about 100 people.

Most of the young crowd cheered when Charney talked about the wonders of cannabis for medicinal purposes, cooking commercial products, and spirituality. But the real cheers were saved for Brother Walter Tucker, one of the leaders of the Church of the Universe and well-known pot promoter.

"We believe (marijuana) is a sacrament and that it should be shared by all." With that, he lit up a joint and encouraged everyone to share.

About 25 people took Tucker up on his offer.

Although police were visible throughout the afternoon, none were around when Tucker and the crowd smoked the illegal weed.

Kitchener Superintendent Brian Koepke with the Waterloo Regional Police visited the festival earlier in the day but said he wasn't too worried about it.

Anti-pot activists wear burlap

"I just wanted to see what's going on," he said with a smile. "Last year it was pretty peaceful."

But he said there were additional officers patrolling the area, and some possibly undercover in the crowd.

He also admitted he could "smell it in the air" but walked away.

Late Sunday, a police spokesman said he was not aware of any charges being laid at the event.

Other members of the community were not as tolerant of the pot party. Erika Kubassek and her husband Phil, local Christian activists, wrapped themselves in burlap. These anti-pot activists wear burlap and tried to convince the crowd that smoking marijuana is wrong.

"I'm sad that people want to mess up their minds and bodies. We are both very sad that people would have to go to delusional drugs to find joy," said Erika.

She said the burlap, or sackcloth, is a traditional sign of mourning from the Bible and she and her husband were mourning society's "departure from the Lord."

Although many didn't agree with the Kubasseks, there was spirited debate wherever they went.

Sarah Anderson, 22 of Waterloo, didn't notice any hostility.

Contrary to New Agers ideas, this religion and the unhealthy drug habit connected with it, are extremely dangerous to the human body, mind and eternal soul, because it opens people to demonic possession, and the destruction of their God-given bodies. And, finally, a fiery hell awaits these deceived souls.

CHAPTER NINE

The Year 2000

We have entered the third millennium and look back to reflect upon two millennia of the "Christian Era" of untold pain, suffering unprecedented bloodshed and gross injustice. But we look forward with great joy and anticipation to the fulfillment of prophecy concerning our Lord's return and His loving rulership together with His saints.

Hosea the prophet says: "After two days He will revive us; on the third day He will restore us, that we may live in His presence." (Hosea 6:2). Scripture says, with the Lord a thousand years are as one day.

In the past, the most horrendous crimes were committed in the name of Christianity – in contrast with Christ's teachings of love. To find answers, we have to look back and see where the Christian church made the pivotal wrong turn away from God's Word unto the path of human understanding. Therefore, we need to follow Christianity's course over the past two millennia. When Jesus' ministry was finished at His death in 33 AD, His apostles spread the Gospel aboard. Christianity traveled through Asia Minor, (now Turkey), and was brought to Rome by the apostles Peter and Paul. In the year 64 AD, the great fire destroyed Rome, and Emperor, Nero, blamed the Christians. They lived in catacombs under the Roman city. Apostles Peter and Paul were martyred, and many Christians died at the hands of the Romans. But, in spite of this severe persecution, the Christian church grew and spread far and wide. By the Middle Ages, however, the teachings of Christ were largely compromised, and the Church, now called the Catholic church, no longer had any resemblance to the early Christian church.

Today, we face another kind of dilemma. Mainline churches blatantly ignore God's law book, the Bible – refusing to obey His laws and commands on vital issues of morality. And, society at large, has banned the Bible from the public domain. Why? There has been no real leadership from the Christian church. It has retreated into the safety behind the walls of their churches, and has not confronted Hollywood and the pornographers. Society now has abandoned the traditional lifestyle in favor of the Hollywood lifestyle of no commitment, free sex, and debauchery.

As we enter the third millenium, we can hear the thundering hooves of the Horsemen of the Apocalypse. Once again, we need men and women who are ready and willing to step forth to declare God's message of repentance and salvation to a world gone awry – to let them know that sexual immorality, the perversion of homosexuality, abortion, greed and cruelty, will shortly bring God's final judgment.

God's messengers must be unafraid to admonish a wicked world as well as encourage the remnant of God's children to persevere and to adhere to God's Word. To love and forgive others, even their enemies, and above all, to love, honor and worship the Lord, our God. Then, and only then, can they have that blessed assurance that God's security system will not fail them, even as the world descends into untold chaos, because underneath God's children are the everlasting arms of God. (Deut. 33:27).

No Vision

On October 18, 2000, the inauguration of the "Women are Persons" monument, celebrating Canadian women as "Nation Builders," took place on Parliament Hill in Ottawa.

Canadian Heritage Minister, Sheila Copps, sent me an invitation to attend this prestigious ceremony on "the Hill," with a reception to follow. Beth, an acquaintance, and I, arrived on a beautiful, crisp, fall day.

White tents were set up for the festivities. I am quite familiar with one of the women being honored as a Nation Builder. Her name is Nellie McClung, who in her life time fought for

Women's right to vote, and was also a member of the Woman's Christian Temperance Union. The monument recognizing the work of five Canadian women, was inaugurated that day.

After speeches from Gov. General Adrienne Clarkson, and others, I had the opportunity to meet Conservative Leader, Joe Clark and his wife, Justice Minister Anne McLellan, Alliance MP Deborah Grey, and finally, Prime Minister, Jean Chretien, and I passed some of my articles on moral issues, to them.

When Mr. Chretien walked over to me to shake hands, I said, "I'm concerned about the moral issues in Canada. I'm a prophetess of the Lord." As he reached out for the envelope I was holding, he had a very incredulous look on his face. Clearly, our message that God exists and still has prophetic servants, surprised him. But, God's methods are the same today as always. God made laws by which man must abide, which continue to be ignored by the Liberal government, as well as the Conservative government.

There is presently no abortion law on the books in Canada, so that the abortion of a baby is tolerated up to the time of birth – and this is, plain and simple – murder. Gay rights and benefits are extended to homosexual and lesbian couples. Pornography, public nudity, and gambling are legal causing family break-up, mental illness, substance abuse, suicides, violence, and murder.

Traditional opinion respecting God's laws, has now been abandoned by the majority of today's society, and any hint of moral responsibility, meets with criticism. Christians who stand for morality are ridiculed, being called bigots or homophobes.

On the Clock Tower of the House of Commons, there is the inscription, "Where there is not vision, the people perish," by Isaiah, the prophet. We have arrived at this sad state of affairs today.

Let's flee Sodom

Up, get out of this place, for the LORD will destroy this city. (Gen. 19:13).

In the biblical account in the book of Genesis, God sent two angels to Lot in Sodom towards the evening, to warn him and his family of the impending doom of Sodom and Gomorrah. These cities were exceedingly immoral – to the point where the inhabitants were ready to seduce even the angels sent by God. Today's morality has pretty well reached the same level of depravity.

Canada has changed some 58 laws to accommodate same-sex relationships, granting the same rights and benefits as to married couples. Gay Pride parades disgrace Canadian and US cities. Toronto hosts one of these Gay Pride parades every year, and its former Mayor, Mel Lastman, participated in it. In a letter, which I was personally able to deliver to Mr. Lastman, and gay city councilor Kyle Rae, with a copy going to the media, read: It is a shame that Mayor Lastman, most of our politicians and the media don't respect God's moral laws. Now, these leaders will be responsible when calamity comes to this nation. Clearly, they don't give moral leadership and are deceiving the people by their participation and acquiescence, into a godless and depraved lifestyle.

The Toronto Sun, dated July 4, 1997, reported that the Metro Police threatened to put a stop to the annual Gay Pride parade. Concerns such as floats featuring bondage stark naked participants sauntering past wide-eyed children watching the Yonge Street spectacle last weekend. Hundreds of thousands of people crowded downtown streets to see bottomless men flaunting their genitals, bound and naked men being tortured with feathers and whips, men with pierced testicles in open view, and leather clad masters whipping and pulling their leashed slaves. It was escalating past the point of fair play ....and common decency.

Erika Kubassek, of the citizens Moral Support Group, sent letters of complaint yesterday to Police Chief David Boothby, Premier Mike Harris, and Attorney-General Charles Harnick. "There's a law on the books and it should be enforced" Kubassek said. "Citizens are extremely offended that this shameless and perverted behavior is tolerated."

But, sadly, the Gay Pride parades were not stopped.

The plague of AIDS affects people who have stepped out of God's moral boundaries. Gay sex and free sex are contrary to God's will for people. Even though many people think they are having fun – let's make no mistake about it, they are flirting with death.

HIV infections are expected to increase dramatically in the next few years. Statistics say that 58 million people have been infected globally, and 22 million have died.
36 million are HIV positive, with the majority in Africa. Canada's HIV/AIDS rate is also increasing.

As Western society continues to outlaw traditional, biblical views – even attempting to ban God's law book, the Bible, – people need not be surprised when God removes His hand of protection and "acts of God" increase. Let's be honest, the handwriting is on the wall.

Once all moral and legal barriers are removed from homosexuality, this change will reach into every family, and touch every person. Our youth, especially, will be detrimentally affected. As articles in homosexual journals show, the seducing of the young is advocated and widespread among homosexuals, and young people are presented with this "alternative" lifestyle in schools today. They can thus be easily sidelined into the homosexual lifestyle.

Further, politically correct principle of "tolerance" towards the gay lifestyle is disastrous for the country; weakening the family further. And, homosexuality is a physically and spiritually dangerous path. Doctors agree that male homosexuals run a particularly high risk of sexually transmitted diseases. It is now known that females as well can infect one another. Homosexuality dramatically shortens the individuals life span. Studies published in the American magazine, 'Fidelity', report that the average age of death of male homosexuals is 42 years. Gays with AIDS die, on average, at the age of 39. Lesbians die at the average age of 45. But, health considerations aside, the moral-spiritual impact of sodomy is even of greater significance. Sadly, people who refuse to repent and continue to break God's moral laws, face a fiery, lost eternity.

The Watchman

"But if the watchman sees the sword coming and does not blow the trumpet to warn the people and the sword comes and takes the life of one of them, that man will be taken away because of his sin but I will hold the watchman accountable for his blood." Like John the Baptist, the LORD commissioned us to "Blow the trumpet in Zion and to warn the people of God's approaching judgment." Like many other servants of God, we were misunderstood in our role, and suffered much persecution.

A letter was written to Brent Hawkes, Minister of the Metropolitan Community Church, with copies to the Toronto, Kitchener, and Cambridge media, as follows.

December 14, 2000.

LETTER WILL BE HAND-DELIVERED ON SUNDAY, DEC. 17th. 2000

TO:
Mr. Brent Hawkes
-and-
The Metropolitan Community Church

It is been reported in the media that you are planning to marry same-sex couples according to an ancient Christian tradition.

The lie, that there are alternative ways of living, rather than how God created us to function, is perpetuated in society and has found its way into some churches – thereby profaning God's house. Homosexuality and lesbianism are disobedience to God's laws. (See Holy Scriptures as follows: Leviticus 20:13, 1.Cor. 6:9, Rom. 1:27.)

Because the Holy Scriptures forbid homosexuality, in fact declare it an abominable sin and because no Christian tradition allows for homosexual marriage, WE STRONGLY PROTEST YOUR ATTEMPT TO PERFORM homosexual or lesbian marriages.

THIS PROTEST IS BINDING UPON YOU AND IF YOU CHOOSE TO IGNORE IT, YOU ARE RESPONSIBLE TO GOD.

From:
Erika Kubassek,
Superintendent of Legislation
WCTU

Gay Weddings? What next?

On January 14th., 2001, gay minister Brent Hawkes of the Metropolitan Community Church of Toronto, was set to perform two gay weddings. After firing off our letter of protest (Dec. 14th.), I had no plans to do anything further. But, when the day of the weddings came, my instructions came from above. In the morning, I received a Word from God: "You are the light of this world." As I meditated on this scripture, the Spirit of God began to speak to me: "Go to Toronto and tell them what the Bible, the Word of God, says about homosexuality." Ready to obey the LORD, I knew however, that this would not be an easy task. After I prayed and accepted the mission, I got in touch with Phil who was out of town that morning, telling him about the message I had received. He agreed to meet me and accompany me to Toronto.

After arriving at our destination, we entered the Metropolitan Community Church and sat in the last row. Although I was somewhat nervous, I knew the Lord would lead me. Brent Hawkes had the congregation sing a song and then invited them up to the front for "anointing for healing" service. Here was my opportunity. Getting up quickly, I went forward with others to the front of the church. Turning, I faced the congregation of several hundred, and said in a loud voice: "Homosexuality is an abomination in God's eyes. You will die," …I was going to add how God created man and woman, but Brent Hawkes cut me short, and stood in front of me yelling and screaming: "Stop! Be quiet. Get out. Go sit down." While pressing down on my shoulder to make me stop, he said these words over and over again. Suddenly, my hand shot up in a reflex motion, giving the gay minister a slight push to get him out of my face. At this moment I had on my mind to finish my sentence: - "God created man and woman for each other," and leave the church. However, then I was attacked from the rear, my arm was twisted up my back. As I went down in excruciating pain, Brent Hawkes' body guard dragged me to the back door of the church, handed me over to the police who charged me with "assault". My shoulder felt as though it had almost been dislocated – I was in bad pain. The police now sent for a paddy wagon and shipped me off to Precinct 55. Amazingly, while on the way to the police station I found myself singing. To the police I said: "Today I have been persecuted for righteousness sake," and actually, it was a privilege to suffer for Christ's sake.

After arriving at the police station, I was interrogated, fingerprinted, photographed, and booked like a criminal. From there I was put into a holding cell and abandoned, which was the most scary part. They locked me up and left. How long would they leave me in this small cell? Thank God, that He was with me anyway. Where was Phil? Stripped of all my rights, I was treated with contempt, though I had done nothing evil. The purpose of the "lock-up" was to give opportunity to have the gay weddings performed without any disturbance. Hence, the police was, in fact, protecting the "illegal" weddings.

Phil waited for me in the lobby, and after several hours in custody, I was finally released.

After this traumatic experience, I drove to Florida the next morning, escaping to Daytona Beach, to visit our relatives. I needed to recuperate both physically and emotionally, from the harrowing experience of falling into the "lions den."

By now, the media had a feeding frenzy. They wrote "Christian activist assaults minister." But, words of support were also heard.

The Record, Kitchener, Ont., Wednesday, February 7, 2001.

LETTER TO THE EDITOR:

Kubassek shows courage

One has to admire Erika Kubassek's zeal to stamp out what all true Christians see as a travesty to God's foundational doctrine, that of marriage between one man and one woman for life.

When one has this commitment to God's truth, one is willing to shove the odd false priest and display some out-of -character behavior to make the point needed.

Kubassek has been accused of violence, but there is a difference between violence and acting out of righteous anger.

Christian churches should be speaking out for the Kubasseks of our society: those who are willing to step out of their comfort zone and live the gospel. Being politically correct is not biblical.

We believe in His holy word, which has been authenticated by the prophecies that have taken place. No other document can make this claim.

All other faiths are partial truths with falsehood woven into them. We cannot afford to settle for half truths. Our salvation depends on following absolute truth.

It took courage for Kubassek to stand up for the gospel of Jesus Christ. She was empowered by the Holy Spirit the day she acted against same-sex marriages and Christians who think she is an embarrassment.

Re: Homosexual Marriage

The militant homosexual lobby, led by Brent Hawkes, gay minister of the Metropolitan Community Church, Toronto, held a so-called "wedding service" that is contrary to biblical teaching which forbids homosexuality. But, this man abused the old Christian custom – "reading the bans."

So far, the federal and provincial governments don't recognize same-sex marriages. But, how long? Our government has caved in on same-sex rights and benefits, and we are all paying, supporting their sinful lifestyle.

It is most shameful that any Christian church, such as the United Church of Canada, some of the Anglican and the Lutheran Churches, have gone soft on homosexuality.

Apostate churches will have to pay a heavy price, because it is not a "human right" to break God's moral laws.

Toronto that was called "the good," has now turned into Toronto, - "the vile" with posters advertising gay bars, - smacking of Sodom and Gomorrah.

History is to a nation, as memory is to an individual. An individual deprived of memory, becomes disoriented and lost, not knowing where he has been or where he is going. Now, Western civilization lost its collective mind and suffers from amnesia, forgetting thousands of years of history concerning God's laws on homosexuality and morality as a whole.

When a nation forgets these moral laws, as ours has done, and when politicians put their stamp of approval upon an immoral lifestyle by participating in the vulgar Gay Pride parades, when laws are passed that encourage this type of perverted behavior, there remains but a moment of grace, before that nation feels the rod of God, as did Sodom and Gomorrah.

Like natural laws, God's moral laws are immutable, and breaking these moral laws, is a prescription for disaster.

From Genesis to Revelation the Bible supports marriage between male and female, and Jesus confirmed the Mosaic law, which are laws given for our protection.

When humans, therefore, have the audacity to change God's moral laws, reveling in perversion and unlawful acts, God must, and will act.

Excerpt from front page, The Record, February 17, 2001.
"Speaking for God in everyday life"

Erika Kubassek says she's a messenger of God.

And because the Lord whispers in her ear; she believes it's OK to burst into political meetings to rant about the agenda, sneak into church services to shout Scripture, and in her spare time decry immoral acts with a bullhorn.

It's OK she believes because she's screaming the word of God.

She's been doing it for 24 years ever since the baptismal waters of the Brethren of Early Christianity Church washed away her Lutheran past and left her a non- denominational born-again Christian.

She believes she received her spiritual gifts in the Ontario village of Washington.

She says she speaks in tongues, languages unknown to average laymen. And she's convinced she has the gifts of revelation and prophecy which let her predict the future.

And that's why Kubassek acts as she does.

So what if the Criminal Code of Canada says interrupting a church service is illegal? She's done it more than once and has never been charged. She believes it's her right.

Yesterday, Kubassek received a different kind of message, from a Toronto provincial court: Return on March 8 to answer to an assault charge.

She was charged last month with assaulting a minister who was about to marry two homosexual couples in a Toronto church.

But the Cambridge resident insists it never happened. She was simply trying to relay the voice of God and stop what she considers an improper wedding.

Kubassek justifies her rebellious nature while sitting in a Cambridge coffee shop recently sipping tea and drawing stares.

At 57 she is a sturdy woman, polite and intelligent. She speaks in a low voice unknown to those who have encountered her during a 'Christian protest.' She waves her hands as she quietly declares her rights, the large silver cross around her neck bouncing with every movement.

Her features are soft and her clothes are shapeless and plain, except her blue fur coat.

But still, patrons look at her:

They stare because on this chilly February day, Kubassek has a tan.

Last month after her latest confrontation, she hopped into her angel-white Cadillac and headed to Florida. She needed to get away to visit family and reflect on the protest that went so wrong.

Kubassek admits going to the front of the church and quoting Scripture, announcing why it's wrong for homosexuals to marry.

Toronto police say the minister tried to speak to her and she assaulted him. Kubassek says the minister yelled at her and a "bouncer" jumped on her and twisted her arm. In the process she says her hand inadvertently brushed the minister's face or shoulder:

Whatever the case, she was charged with assault. Kubassek, the self-proclaimed Prophetess of the Lord, was handcuffed and placed in a police cell.

She was hoping to have the charge dropped yesterday, leaving her with a clean record.

But she quickly realized, as she approached the front of the College Park court room in her light pink dress suit, that wasn't going to happen.

The only thing Kubassek left with was a notice to appear.

Rough Treatment

She now plans to hire a full time lawyer. In her mind, she is the one who was the victim of rough treatment in the Toronto church.

"It took time for me to come to grips with it. I've never been treated like that," she says, her German accent still apparent.

Kubassek came to Canada from Germany with her parents in 1957. She was born Erika Kretschmann, the daughter of a Baptist father and Lutheran mother. She was baptized Lutheran, but since a "baby cannot believe" she didn't hesitate to switch religions as an adult.

She grew up in Burlington and Hamilton and took business courses at a community college expecting a career in office work.

But then things changed.

At the age of 32 she went with her father to the Brethren of Early Christianity Church.

"I could see the love of Christ there," she says.

It was there she met Phil Kubassek who also possessed solid Christian values. He caught her eye.

"We were very dedicated," she says. "We wanted to do what was good in God's eyes."

Erika and Phil, part of the Kubassek contracting and development family, dated for about two years. While courting they shared "nothing more than a shy kiss," she says, laughing at the thought of pre-marital sex, something forbidden to the traditional Christian couple.

Kubassek, her face unpainted by makeup, blushes and smiles behind strands of light brown hair as she describes her relationship with Phil. She was engaged once before prior to committing herself to a life of Christianity. But with Phil she knew it was right.

The two married, moved to Kitchener and decided early on not to have children, figuring at 34 she was too old.

But they didn't need children. They had something just as absorbing – a religious conviction that has sent them to churches throughout the region to protest.

Although Kubassek believes her husband also has spiritual gifts, they're not as powerful or used as much as hers.

Hears God

She hears God speak in an audible voice through her spirit almost daily – in the morning, afternoon, evening, whenever He sees fit.

Throughout the years Kubassek says He has sent her to visit political figures such as Jean Chretien, Mike Harris, and Bill Clinton with her messages – love God and your neighbours and live a morally clean life according to the Bible.

In 1992 God told her to travel across the country with a balloon attached to her vehicle that read Canada Return to Christian Values or You Will Fail. She stopped in every major city relaying that message. It took her 30 days.

In 1982, He told her to work for the YMCA so she opened a small shelter for homeless women. But too much work and not enough money forced her to close the shelter within three years and seek medical attention.

She believes stress forced her heart to stop beating one day causing her to lose consciousness. There was only one thing left to do. Pray.

"Lord please give me a second chance" she pleaded.

Almost immediately, she says her silenced heart began to beat.

Too frail to walk she used a wheelchair for six years. Then suddenly she was able to walk again.

It may have been a weak heart caused by overwork that put her in the chair. But it was the Lord she says, who lifted her out of it.

And in a way, these are the miracles that oblige her to relay His messages.

"People wonder why I do this," says Kubassek, who knows some people are annoyed with her holier-than-thou attitude.

"I love people and don't want them going to hell. It's not hatred," she says. "It's tough love."

So how does a woman full of Christian values and love for her neighbours draw national scrutiny?

Pretty easily, say some.

Last summer she was banned from the Ontario Legislature for throwing letters citing homosexuality as one of the causes of the E.coli outbreak in Walkerton.

Those who have seen Kubassek in action weren't surprised. All it takes is a slight sway from God's will to hear the bullhorn protests of the Christian crusader.

Kubassek has never been charged with interrupting a church service, considered a form of disorderly conduct by the justice system.

Toronto police could have charged her with it after the protest last month but opted to lay the more significant charge of assault.

When it comes time, Kubassek will tell her side, feeling confident the charge will be dropped. She just hopes the judge isn't a homosexual activist.

She's decided God wants her to get legal counsel since friends had given her names of local Christian lawyers. That was a sign, she figures.

And though she isn't expecting Him to just drop money at her doorstep she knows the Lord will find a way to pay her legal bills.

Firm Path

Convicted or not, Kubassek has no plans to change her lifestyle. No person pastor or religion can stop her message.

My Court Case

"The wicked watch for the righteous, and seek to kill them. The LORD will not abandon them to their power, or let them be condemned when they are brought to trial." (Ps. 37:32-33.)

After several court appearances and a preliminary hearing, I was told that there would be no repercussions and no fine, if only I would plead "Guilty." But how could I plead guilty when I knew in my heart that I had obeyed God in this matter? I could not. I informed my lawyer, Mr. DeMarco of Toronto, that I would plead "Not Guilty." A court date of December 19, 2001, was given to me.

Another private charge of "disturbing a church service" was thrown at me in the summer of 2001 by the Metropolitan Community Church, stemming from the same incident.

Court case delayed for Christian crusader,
Cambridge Times,
August 28, 2001.

Charged with disturbing service at church where gay couple was to wed.

Erika Kubassek will have to wait until Sept. 24 to plead not guilty to a charge of disturbing a service at a Toronto Church where a gay couple was to be married.

Kubassek appeared in court on Thursday but her case was remanded until next month. She said she will plead not guilty.

The Christian crusader was charged on Jan. 14 after she attended a service at the Metropolitan Community Church and spoke out against gay and lesbian marriages.

A gay couple was to be married at the same church later that day.

She was also charged with assault following a confrontation with the church's minister, Brent Hawkes. That charge goes to court on Dec. 19.

"It is my Christian right and duty to speak out against the sin of homosexuality and gay marriage," Kubassek said in a release. "The so-called minister, Brent Hawkes, and the Metropolitan Community Church of Toronto, are guilty of blasphemy by asking God to bless sinful gay marriages."

On December 19, 2001, Phil and I entered the Toronto court room accompanied by Pastor Dale Hoch of International Gospel Center in Kitchener. Pastor Dale came to court that day as a character witness. He knew us for approximately twenty years.

In the past I attended I.G.C. (International Gospel Center) and also helped Pastor Dale in outreach ministry during the early 80's. My lawyer, Anthony DeMarco, was also present. When the proceedings were about to begin, I noticed Brent Hawkes, the gay minister was sitting in his black robes with a party of supporters surrounding him on the other side of the court room. His bodyguard, Tony Bryant, was there as well. The lawyers called witness after witness and the picture of what happened, began to emerge. There was one flaw: Brent Hawkes and his group were not telling the truth. They ended up contradicting each other's testimony, which was to my advantage. Thank God, our prayers were being answered in the court hearing. When I took the stand, I told what had transpired, and spoke out against homosexuality – how it is an abomination in God's eyes. I testified how God commanded me to warn the Metropolitan Community Church congregation of the dire consequences to this life style, but that I never intended to touch or hurt anyone.

Pastor Dale and Phil gave me much support in this hearing. Justice William Horkins' decision came on January 22, 2002: "Not guilty." How faithfully the LORD defended me. Some details are as follows:

My reasons for judgment in this case then, this is a charge of assault, said Judge Horkins. Ms. Kubassek attended Reverend Hawkes' church here in Toronto on January the 14th. of last year and she ended up going up to the front of the church to address the congregation. At that point she was confronted by Reverend Hawkes. She pushed him out of the way. There was no serious physical consequence at the time and she was summarily removed.

I find as a fact here, having considered all of the evidence that Ms. Kubassek did not go to that church with the intention of assaulting anybody.

I have considered the character evidence called on her behalf and the evidence that she gave on her own behalf and I am quite satisfied that she is a person of good character, that her firmly held beliefs include a pacifist approach and there is nothing in the evidence that would persuade me otherwise than that she felt compelled by her beliefs to go there and do something. I am quite satisfied on the totality of the evidence that she had not formulated in her own mind exactly what it was that she was going to do. I am satisfied that she had not decided to go there with the intention of assaulting anyone. Her purpose in going there is just one aspect, one characteristic of the entire transaction.

However, I think it is fair to say that no one would characterize her conduct as, to use the perhaps old fashioned words of some of the cases, as "cloaked in criminality." Here is a woman who is driven by her very firmly held religious beliefs to speak out against something that to her is shocking and appalling. I do not make any finding that she went there to purposely trigger a demonstration or disturbance. I suspect very much in fact, and I accept her evidence, that she did not know what she was going to do until the opening presented itself, when people were invited by Reverend Hawkes to come to the front. This invitation inspired her, at that very moment, to go forward and speak out. There was no more degree of planning or preparation than that in what she did.

The next characteristic that is significant in these sort of situations is the duration of the contact, the results of the physical contact, and the spontaneity of the physical contact. There is no mystery in this case that this was extremely brief contact. It was transient. There were no injuries. The consequences were minor and passing. Not that they could not have easily caused some injury, but in fact, there were minor and transient. And the spontaneity of it, although not reflexive, bordered on it.

Now, having said that, to make it clear that I have that aspect of it in my mind, I look at the history of the 'de minimus" concept as it is applied and I try to grasp what the law considers to be "trifling?" I appreciate that applying the word trifling" in this case has the risk of offending Reverend Hawkes at least, for me to say that this was "trifling." It may be that in everyday language, that could be an inaccurate description. But in the context of the criminal law this conduct was "trifling." It was rude. It was offensive. And it was definitely the wrong thing to do. It is "trifling" in the larger scheme of criminal conduct. In all of the circumstances and looking at the different aspects of it, this conduct was incidental and of such a minor degree that in the particular circumstances of the case there can not be a finding of criminal liability. I am not going to find the accused guilty or convict her of the offence.

The reason that I have gone on at some length, is I hope, although it is not a bright line, to illustrate that this case is quite distinguishable from those where someone goes somewhere to cause trouble, knows that it causes trouble and bashes on regardless. I expressly find that that was not the case here. For all of those reasons the charge will be dismissed.

A subsequent appeal by Brent Hawkes was defeated.

'Messenger of God' not guilty of assaulting Toronto minister, The Record, January 23, 2002.

Minutes after being found not guilty of assaulting a Toronto pastor, Erika Kubassek did what every self-proclaiming messenger of God would do.

She praised the Lord.

"This is wonderful," she said as she walked out of a Toronto courtroom yesterday.

"Praise God."

The outspoken Cambridge woman, known for her bull-horn protests against what she believes to be anti-Christian behavior, was charged with assaulting Rev. Brent Hawkes and disturbing a church service at Toronto's Metropolitan Community Church on Jan. 14, 2001.

She was found not guilty on the assault charge, but will have to return to court on Feb. 6 to speak to the disturbance charge, which was laid privately by the church last July.

Kubassek was charged after going to the front of the church during an 11 A.M. service and denouncing homosexuality.

A well-publicized marriage ceremony for two same-sex couples, using the Christian tradition of publishing banns, occurred later that afternoon.

Court heard that Kubassek pushed Hawkes after he tried to quiet her as she shouted Scripture at the front of the church. She said she had received a message from God telling her to go to the church and speak out against homosexuality.

She arrived at court yesterday with a friend and both bowed their heads in prayer before the proceedings started.

An issue was whether Kubassek had the criminal intent to assault Hawkes when she pushed him away.

Justice William Horkins said although Kubassek "exhibited extreme, rude judgment," she didn't go to the church with thoughts of assaulting someone. He added that the assault was considered "trifling" by law, the conduct was incidental and to such a minor degree, that Kubassek should be found not guilty.

During her trial last month, Kubassek spoke out against the homosexual unions, calling it "an abomination and a sin in God's eyes."

Yesterday, she said she'll continue to speak out against the lifestyle.

When asked if she would ever disrupt a church service again, Kubassek said "sure," but that she would "be very careful not to put a finger on someone."

The gay church appealed Justice Horkins' decision later, but lost their appeal. The other charge was dropped.

To The Editor,
The Cambridge Times, January 25, 2002.
Erika Kubassek does it by the 'book'

I'm writing in regards to the Erika Kubassek incident, initially, I'd like to confirm that any jeering of the woman or desperate accusations of fanaticism should not come as a surprise to anyone who has ever studied the Bible. Jesus said that people would hate his followers because they don't want their own deeds to be exposed. Jesus was not one to cower in the corner quietly when he was confronted with injustice, and neither should his followers be. Anyone who believes in the validity of the Bible or dares to call themselves a Christian should be in full support of Erika's position. There is no argument to be had regarding God's opinion on homosexuality, that's always been clear. And if you want to forego the Scripture and move to a more obvious indicator of such, I invite you to ponder the fact that we were created to be man and woman together.

Don't ask me which way I want my eggs done when I've already made myself some scrambled. Hear what I'm saying? So stand up, strap on some courage and be appalled at the "Reverend" Brent Hawkes for violating God's word in His own house.

By the way, save your breath and don't write a reply accusing me of "homophobia," promoting hate crimes or anything else you can come up with. Neither what you say, or what I think matters, God has said what He has said.

In June 2003, the Ontario Appeal's Court in Toronto, announced that Gay Marriages are now legal. Radio 570 in Kitchener, asked me to comment on these developments. I promptly denounced the homosexual lifestyle and gay marriage, warning that serious consequences will follow. My letter to the editor on this subject went into the local newspapers as follows:

Society loses standards,
The Record, June 14, 2003.

Canada ought to be in mourning after the catastrophic judicial decision by the Ontario Appeals Court in Toronto to allow gay marriage. What are these judges thinking?

From a moral and spiritual stand-point, this decision is a disaster; if it is allowed to stand. It means the death of the family, as God intended it to be.

It seems that decency and morality are no longer treasured. Society no longer has standards and descends ever further into the quagmire of moral decay.

History shows us that amoral societies met with disaster: It should come as no surprise then if pestilence, disasters and finally the destruction of our society will be the result.

Fulfillment of Prophecies

I was asked to go on the 'Paul and Carol Mott Show on CFRB Radio, in Toronto, in the early part of June/03. The subject was 'end – time' prophecy and my calling in particular. Since the scary 'SARS' plague, the Mad Cow outbreak, and the danger of West Nile virus infection, dominated the news, they asked me if these plagues are God's punishment. I told them that we went on record in 2001 and 2002 warning about gay marriage, abortion, and immorality in general. We witnessed to the Metropolitan Church, Ontario Court, and many in the media about God's moral laws. Sadly, they continue to ignore our prophetic ministry. As a matter of fact, the Ontario Appeals Court in Toronto, has now legalized same sex marriages. I told Paul and Carol that the Lord is definitely sending judgment because of today's moral decay. Their reaction was subdued and I could tell they were asking questions in their own hearts. May God convict the hosts and listeners of the program, so that they would seek the way of Salvation and uphold God's moral standards.

CHAPTER TEN

Cloning – The Last Straw

We are already being used as guinea pigs in a giant experiment with genetically modified food. In view of the fact that science and technology has given us mega pollution, unsafe drugs, dangerous hormones (DES), harmful pesticides, denatured food, the atomic bomb, Chernobyl, biological, chemical warfare, and other assorted disasters. Since the fact that cancer rates are through the roof, there is serious concern now about what bio foods may do to people, animals, and the environment. Further, the scientific community, which gave us test tube babies with in-vitro-fertilization, is now busy cloning animals, and perhaps, humans next.

In 2002, Italian doctor, Severino Antinori, claimed that a woman was pregnant with a cloned baby. Later, the New Age group the "Raeliens" of Quebec, announced that a cloned baby was born at the end of 2002. There was, however, no scientific proof presented of this occurrence. Never-the-less, this shows that there is interest in this perverted science of cloning, and that it is only a matter of time when someone will be successful in producing a human clone.

Animal cloning has already been done, but the famous sheep "Dolly," only survived six years – half the life span of her breed. So far, human cloning has been outlawed. Yet, the scientific community always seems to push the 'envelope.' Why do the scientists insist on tampering with God's creation? Why do they want to be "like God?" Is it not because of the love of money and fame? In their presumption and pride, they continue to intrude on God's territory – his creative realm.

The complexity of living organisms, their DNA, RNA, and genes speak of God's awesome creative power and wisdom.

Why would mere mortals dare to interfere?

When materialism or pride, instead of love and concern for the whole human family, fuel scientific and technological endeavor, there is little hope that disaster can be averted.

Indeed, when money drives morality – the people are in jeopardy.

The Bible says: "The love of money is the root of all evil."

Let's make no mistake about it, if God allowed the current trend to continue, the next generations would inherit a mixed-up, surreal, perverted, and morally corrupt world.

Noah was God's witness to the people of his time.

When the earth's inhabitants corrupted themselves beyond reason, God was sorry that he had created them and He decided to wipe them off the face of the earth, with the flood, except for Noah and his family.

In the end, God will have no choice but to send the fires of Armageddon to cleanse the earth from all wickedness.

Is Armageddon Near?

And they gathered them together into a place called in Hebrew, "Armageddon." (Rev. 16:16). Lord, how long shall the wicked triumph? (Ps. 94:3.)

The word "Armageddon" is used to describe the end of the world by fire, but it is also a place in Israel. It is called the "Valley of Megiddo", not far from the border of the occupied West Bank. This region is the very heart of Bible prophecy.

In September of 2002, I received a prophetic message in a spiritual vision. I saw a red horse, in the spirit, and the LORD spoke to me, "The red horse is riding." I immediately went to the biblical book of Revelation and read: "When the Lamb opened the second seal, I heard the second living creature say, "Come!" Then another horse came out, a fiery red one. Its rider was given power to take peace from the earth and to make men slay each other, to him was given a large sword. (Rev. 6:3).

Since that time, war has claimed many lives. The violence in Israel and the war in Iraq are the matches that ignite the powder keg of the Middle East – eventually exploding into the third World War, culminating with Armageddon. It has been reported that the Pentagon was given permission to launch nuclear strikes against enemies that use biological, chemical or nuclear weapons. Rogue states that countries like Iran, North Korea, Libya, Syria, may try to do just that. Nuclear proliferation daily increases the danger of nuclear war. Another trouble spot in the world is India and Pakistan who have nuclear capabilities and are bitter enemies. Several times they almost pushed the nuclear button. Relations with Russia and China have become more strained lately as well. So clearly, the world has become a much more dangerous place.

There exists a doomsday clock that the Atomic Scientists of Chicago keep adjusting according to the danger of nuclear conflict in the world. It is now, but a few minutes to mid-night. Considering the evidence of conflicts, plagues, and disasters, we hear the thundering hoof beats of the Apocalypse, and God's warning to a sinful world. Today's headlines scream of war, terrorism, killer viruses, radically changing weather patterns, earth quakes, famines, destruction, and death. They are all harbingers of the terrible "Day of the LORD."

The biblical book of Revelation states further: "Then the kings of the earth, the princes, the generals, the rich, the mighty, and every slave, and every free man, hid in caves and among the rocks of the mountains. They called to the mountains and the rocks: "Fall on us and hide us from the face of Him who sits on the throne and from the wrath of the Lamb!" "For the great day of their wrath has come, and who can stand?" (Rev. 6:15).

The world has had its last chance. Now they are arming for Armageddon. Bible prophecy is rapidly coming to pass before our very eyes. The remnant of true Christians are called to declare God's message that the sexual immorality, the perversion of homosexuality, the abortions, the New Age demon worship, the greed and cruelty, will bring God's final judgment.

In antiquity, before Jerusalem fell to the Roman legions in 70 AD, the Jews ignored God's loud warning signs. According to Jewish historian, Flavius Josephus, (Josephus,

Thrones of Blood, Barbour), there were preceding signs of Jerusalem's destruction. Also, prior to the destruction, there came a man by the name of Jesus, son of Annanus (not the Christ), who brought a prophecy of doom to the city of Jerusalem. He went about day and night proclaiming: A voice from the rising, a voice from the setting, a voice from the four winds, and a voice over Jerusalem, a voice over all the people. And he called out: "Woe, woe Jerusalem." Many times he was beaten, but he continued to proclaim his message. His prophecy continued for seven years and five months. As the Roman armies approached Jerusalem, and as he yelled loudly, "Woe to the city, the people and the temple," a flying stone silenced him, and he died with God's message on his lips. So God warned the people, but they would not listen to the prophet's warning, and were destroyed because of their foolishness. Jesus Christ foretold the destruction of Jerusalem. He knew the heart of man.

Many prophecies have now been fulfilled. Jesus said: "When you see all these things, recognize that He is near, right at the door." (Matt. 24:33) The signs of Jesus imminent return are everywhere, and just as Jesus' prophecy came to pass in 70 AD, when Jerusalem and the temple were razed to the ground, so will all the other prophecies come to pass.

There is, however, the blessed assurance that as judgment looms, God's security system will not fail those who repent and follow Jesus.

Israel's Promise

We are commanded to pray for the peace of Jerusalem. (Ps. 122: 6)

When Ex-Prime Minister, Benjamin Netanjahu, visited Toronto in the late 1990's, he spoke at the Harbour Castle Conference Center, with hundreds in attendance. I had the opportunity to be there as well. The Jewish business community was out in full force to hear Mr. Netanjahu speak. Ontario Premier Mike Harris, sat on the stage with Mr. Netanjahu and his wife, Sara.

Mr. Netanjahu's speech centered on the subject of "Peace for Israel." He quoted Moses and the Philosopher, Emmanuel Kant, outlining his vision for peace in Israel. Now with his address delivered and lunch finished, he invited people to the microphone for questions. I immediately popped up from my chair and made my way to the front of the large conference room where the mike stood. "Mr. Netanjahu," I said, "I heard you mention Moses and Emmanuel Kant, but I did not hear you mention Jesus Christ, the Prince of Peace." I then briefly witnessed how Jesus had given me the wonderful miracle of healing me and lifting me from that dreadful wheelchair. I also quoted Jesus' recipe for peace: "Love your enemies." Clearly, only love will overcome evil.

After I had finished my short witness, Mr. Netanjahu answered and said: "Thank you for your faith. Yes, I know that the evangelical Christians are on Israel's side." I stepped aside now, to let the next person have the floor. Full of joy I walked back to my table, knowing that everybody was staring at me in surprise. I knew that I had fulfilled my mission, and God's Holy Spirit had spoken through my mouth to many hearts.

When Mr. Netanjahu was still Prime Minister of Israel, I wrote him an encouraging letter and the following was his reply:

Letter received from the Prime Minister's Office, July 10, 1997.

Dear Mr. and Mrs. Kubassek,

On behalf of Prime Minister Benjamin Netanyahu, thank you for your letter of May 8, 1997, and kind words of encouragement and support.

The basic guidelines of our government state our strong belief in the Jewish People's unquestionable right to the Land of Israel. The Government is firmly opposed to the establishment of an independent Palestinian State, and insists that Jerusalem remains united as the eternal, undivided capital of Israel.

We will continue to strive for peace with our neighbors based on the principles of signed agreements, and our conviction that we have the right to live securely in the Land of our Fathers.

Your concern is much appreciated and your views and proposals have been duly noted.

With warm greetings from Jerusalem,

From the office of Prime Minister Benjamin Netanyahu.

In the New Testament, we are told that God did not reject His people Israel. Their blindness of heart, a result of their unbelief, would be removed in the time of the end. But, only a remnant of Jewish people is chosen by God's grace. (Rom. 11:5) Who are they? They are those who still hope in God and accept Jesus as their Messiah. God will lead His people, Israel, down into the Valley of Achor, which means the valley of deep suffering, in order to bring them to repentance.

When Jesus Christ was crucified, the veil of the temple was rent in two, opening up the Holy of Holies. Now there was access to God for all who accepted Jesus, through the atoning sacrifice of the Lamb of God. It is said that there is a passage in the Jewish Talmud, written by rabbis who lived in Jesus time, that apparently after Jesus' crucifixion, God no longer accepted animal sacrifices for the sin of the people in the temple, until the temple was razed to the ground in 70 AD by Roman armies.

Letter to:

February 19, 2002.

Prime Minister Ariel Sharon,
The Knesset,
Jerusalem, Israel

Dear Prime Minister Sharon:

Sadly, Israel has been ravaged with war and terrorism for many years now. We wish to express our sincere sorrow at the bloodshed and violence perpetrated in the region and for the plight of the Jewish people.

Please, be assured that we pray for Israel and in particular for Jerusalem every single day. It belongs to the LORD GOD OF

ISRAEL. May the Temple be built very soon and the mosques be eliminated, we pray.

There is one stipulation for Peace for Israel. It needs to accept the Prince of Peace, Jesus Christ – the Messiah.

The Prophet Isaiah says in Isaiah 53: "But He was wounded for our transgressions, He was bruised for our iniquity; the chastisement of our P E A C E was upon Him; and with His stripes we are healed."

"For He was cut off out of the land of the living; for the transgression of MY PEOPLE was He stricken. By His knowledge shall my RIGHTEOUS SERVANT justify many, for He shall bear their iniquities."

"Adam's sin of disobedience to the LORD GOD was removed by JESUS' obedience unto death – and we were reconciled to the LORD GOD of Abraham." (Rom. 5: 18.)

So far the Jewish nation has a veil over their eyes and heart, BUT THIS VEIL SHALL BE REMOVED IN TRIBULATION AND WHEN THERE IS NO HELPER, BUT JESUS CHRIST, ISRAEL WILL MOURN OVER JESUS AS FOR AN ONLY SON.

Then Israel will be set free!

Pray and seek the LORD'S face and read the New Testament which contains wonderful promises for Israel.

In the meantime, we will continue to pray that God's people Israel, will come into the glorious freedom of the Son of God.

CHAPTER ELEVEN

God's Kingdom is coming!

If those terrible days of Armageddon were not shortened, no flesh would survive.(Matt. 24:22.)

But, thank God, Jesus will intervene and cut short the battle between good and evil. It is prophesied that His return with His saints shall bring restoration to the earth. When the smoke has cleared and all evil been subdued, once again, the earth will return to be like the beautiful Garden of Eden. The LORD then confines Satan and his cohorts to the bottomless pit for a thousand years. God removes the curse from the earth and people, as well as animals, heave a sigh of relief. They will once again enjoy a long healthy life in a restored earth. The lion will lie down with the lamb, and no one will make them afraid or destroy them anymore. (Isaiah 11: 6-10.)

Jubilation shall break forth all over when freedom from the oppressive, demonic evil forces is finally a reality.

How can you be saved

When asking people if they are saved, they reply: "Saved from what?"

They don't realize that because of Adam's disobedience to God, sin came upon all of mankind and their nature became marred, separating them from God. The whole human family needs a Saviour, because man is unable to keep God's holy laws. Animal sacrifices are insufficient. Salvation originates in God's holy heart, and so, He had a plan to save the world through His Son, Jesus.

By repentance and acceptance of the sacrifice of Jesus, by trusting in Jesus as their Saviour, through the cross of Calvary, the way opens for man to return to God. Sin came by one man. Salvation comes by one man, Jesus. He is the road back to God's heart. Salvation is the only answer to our sinful, helpless, hopeless condition.

The plan of salvation involves a total change in direction. We must come to recognize what sin is, to hate it, and to repent. Our loving Saviour saves us, cleanses us from our fallen, vile nature, and brings us back to fellowship with God, the Father. The cleansing process is painful; the way of the cross is necessary because God says: Be ye holy as I am holy. The old, sinful nature MUST be put to death, so that the new nature, born of the Holy Spirit, can arise to give us the image of Christ. Now that is radical. Yes, God has to purge us from our character flaws.

In John Bunyan's book published in 1678, called the "Pilgrim's Progress," the pilgrim called "Christian" is exhorted to leave the City of Destruction, and travel to the Celestial City. Life is pictured as a journey through many trials and temptations. Christian through obedience to God's Word and Spirit, perseveres, and finally arrives in the Heavenly Jerusalem to be with God forever.

The Bible says: He that believes (in Jesus) and is baptized, the same shall be saved. (Mark 16:16). The believers' baptism is an essential step of obedience and seals the believer with the Holy Spirit of God.

Are you ready? I invite you to pray the sinner's prayer as follows: Lord Jesus, I believe You are the Son of God. I believe that You died for me. I repent of my sins. I ask You to please forgive me and come into my heart. Save my soul. Thank you Lord. So my friend, let the main thing, be the main thing – the main thing **IS** your salvation.

The Person of Christ
By Philip Schaff.

The Historian Philip Schaff outlined the overwhelming influence which the life of Jesus of Nazareth had on subsequent history and culture of the Western World. "This Jesus of Nazareth without money and arms, conquered more millions then Alexander, Caesar,

Mohammed, and Napolean; without science and learning He shed more light on things human and divine than all philosophers and scholars combined; without eloquence of schools, He spoke such words of life as were never spoken before or since, and produced effects which lie beyond the reach of orator or poet; without writing a single line, He set more pens in motion, and furnished themes for more sermons, orations, discussions, learned volumes, works of art, and songs of praise than the whole army of great men of ancient and modern times."

One of our relatives, who was a missionary, writes this: **Somebody does love you unconditionally**

There is a love far beyond our human limitations. To find true love we must look outside of ourselves. By our own experience we know how changeable we can be and how incapable we are to love in many circumstances.

There is some one who's very nature and essence is Divine Love.

Even if you don't know it, this love has already been extended to you personally. Jesus Christ, the Son of God, proved that he loves you and every other human being who ever lived on this planet. "But God demonstrates His own love toward us, in that while we were still sinners, Christ died for us." (Rom. 5:8.) Every person has committed offenses worthy of punishment in hell, but Jesus stepped forward and said "I will pay the price so humanity can go free." There isn't any greater expression of love than if a person is willing to lay down his or her life for a friend. Jesus went a lot further than that when He died, in love, for the very ones who hated Him and nailed Him to a cross. The fact is that we are guilty of His death until we receive his pardon. Regardless of how good or bad we may consider ourselves, every one of us is condemned unless we are willing to accept God's loving forgiveness. "And we are being cleansed from every sin by the blood of Jesus His Son." (1 John 1:7.)

A Changed Life

This is your opportunity to have a changed life and to enjoy all the benefits **God has provided for those who love Him. Just**

talk to God and tell Him how you are feeling. Ask Him to help you believe in Him and to forgive all your sins. Promise God that with his help, you will live the rest of your life for Him. Now you can thank God that He has heard your prayer, and that He will never leave you. God's Holy Spirit will come to dwell in you and will enable you to know and do, what is right.

Once Christ Jesus is believed upon and accepted, we become born again. This birth is in the spiritual dimension and it means we are born into the family of God as his own children. As the children of God we inherit the nature of God. It now becomes possible to love others, and God, even as he also loves us. We will find it a joy to do what is right, and look for opportunities to share our life-transforming experience. As we continue our walk with the LORD there are many experiences which will help us develop into a state of Christ-like maturity. Most definitely **YOU ARE LOVED,** and you **BELONG!** The family of God encompasses the globe, and by God's grace you are a very special member. Following is the Bible's definition of the kind of love God has for His own and as His children we are able to show Him and others.

"Love is patient; love is kind and envies no one. Love is never boastful, nor conceited, nor rude; never selfish, not quick to take offense. Love keeps no score of wrongs; does not gloat over other men's sins, but delights in the truth. There is nothing love cannot face; there is no limit to its faith, its hope, and its endurance." (1Cor. 13:4-7)

To love God you must know Him. To get to know Him, you must read His Word, the Bible, whether it is by hearing or reading. Can you have a relationship with the God of the Bible? You certainly can. Are you ready to fight the good fight of faith? Then be prepared to do battle with the evil forces of the devil.

To ignore God's loving call to salvation would invite disaster into your life, and you will live with eternal regret. Jesus is the same yesterday, today and forever, He still saves, heals and sends today – a much better choice for you.

THE WARNING

Bible prophecies are coming to pass at an ever-faster pace. We are in the "Days of the Apocalypse." What is next?

There will be an increase, as well as more severe "Acts of God." They include weather-related catastrophes, pestilence, war, wild-fires, and other grave disasters. According to the Holy Scriptures, we have entered the time period called "the tribulation."

It was revealed to Phil and I that the Walkerton water contamination catastrophe, the SARS outbreak in Toronto, the Mad Cow scare, the drought in the West, and severe wild-fires in British Columbia, are indeed punishments from the LORD. God's arm is hammering the US, and recently, Europe lost 20,000 people to a killer heat wave.

When governments and populations blatantly break God's laws contained in God's Word, the Bible, by abortion, legalizing homosexuality and gay marriage, prostitution, strip clubs and rampant immorality, when divorce is at epidemic rates, greed and consumerism is encouraged, occult New Age religion accepted and practiced by multi-millions. When today's paganized, undisciplined youth are taking drugs, being sexually immoral, listening to demonic music and watching wicked lewd films, piercing and tattooing their faces and bodies, and vulgar four letter words and blasphemies come from their mouths - they are called the "lost" generation; when violence is condoned in sports and entertainment, it's no wonder that God's wrath is kindled against Canada, the US, Europe, and the free Western world. Why? Because they know better. They have been built upon biblical laws and values, and are now rejecting these foundations. How can these countries expect to be blessed when they don't respect God's laws any longer? In the US, the Ten Commandments were removed from a courthouse in Alabama, signifying that they no longer serve the LORD. This, sadly, sums up the state of affairs today.

The LORD, in His mercy, sends messengers to warn of judgment to come and we His prophets, are not well received. In old –Israel it was no different. The Jews stoned and killed many prophetic servants because they did not want to listen; they were too stiff-necked to repent, and would not stop their lawless ways. The same is true today, the so-called Christian nations no longer adhere to Christian laws. But will they listen? Not so far. We have warned the leaders of the Western world for a dozen years, and now, the time is very short.

God's warning of coming judgment goes out through His servants, the prophets, - but will the people pay heed before the coming of the "Day of the Lord," when He will judge all flesh?

Next, a powerful leader will arise. He will appear to bring peace to the Middle East and the world. He will have answers to today's problems and people will follow him. He will be "Evil Incarnate" – declaring himself "a god". That is not far-fetched when we listen to New Agers who declare themselves "gods and goddesses" in the media.

This "god" will compel everyone to accept a number perhaps on a microchip, in their bodies. This "Number of the Beast," mentioned in the Book of Revelation, will make people the property of Satan. No one will be able to buy or sell without this number. With security concerns because of terrorism, the computer, will now be employed to keep track of people. On a recent Christian TV program, it was discussed that the US Government is considering micro-chipping all it's citizens. Sadly, most people will go along with this plan because it sounds so reasonable, and after all, they are told it is for their protection. Nothing could be further from the truth. Under no circumstances should people take this number. It will automatically make them Satan's pawns, and will land them in hell, separated from God. (Rev. 13:16, Rev. 14: 9-11).

All those who trust in Jesus have nothing to fear. Even if God allows for them to pass from this life on earth, He surely will take care of them. The Bible says:
"Blessed are the dead who die in the LORD from now on." "Yes," says the Spirit, they will rest from their labour, and their deeds will follow them." (Rev. 14: 13). Obedient Christians who love the Lord, however, can count on God's deliverance and help in times of trouble; for them it's always a 'win-win' situation.

In the Bible, Jesus talks about the parable of the ten virgins, - five were wise and five were foolish. Perhaps, it was only "One Moment to Midnight" when they all went to meet the bridegroom. But, still, there were five who were not ready. They did not have the Holy Spirit. "At midnight, when the bridegroom came, all the virgins went out to meet him but five were wise and five were foolish. The foolish virgins didn't have enough-(Holy Spirit), and their lamps went out. And when they called to the LORD to let them in, He said: Verily, verily I say unto you: I know you not." The other five, the wise Virgins, went into the wedding feast (Matt. 25 6-10).

My words in this book echo the prophet's words: "When all these things come pass and they surely will, you will know that a prophet has been among you." (Ezekiel 33:33).